Poetic Reflections

Poems by

Christine Burrows

Front cover:
**Created with two photographs
superimposed and designed
by the Author**

Notes: compiled by the Author.
All characters and events in this publication,
other than those clearly in the public domain,
are fictitious and any resemblance to real persons,
living or dead, is purely coincidental.

All Rights Reserved.
ISBN-9798876965547
MMXXIV

A Poem . . .

A poem has the power to reform,
to touch the heart and soul, and chill the bone;
to shake foundations with its artful form--
and soothe with words that smell of sweet cologne.

A poem infiltrates the coldest mind
with truth, with facts, it tells a tale of sorrow--
with clever rhymes, a line that's well designed,
can promise that there is a new tomorrow.

A poem lingers long inside our head,
repeating with its clever observation;
until we can't forget what has been said,
with lyrical, melodic validation.

A poem can deliver loving notes,
without a sound, the reader hears a song,
in silence every syllable invokes--
a place where we feel safe and we belong.

A poem to identify emotion,
where all of us have been, and know the ride,
with written words remaining here unspoken,
a poem reaches people far and wide.

I dedicate this book to:
My Father

Author's Preface:

In this collection of over 370 short rhyming poems, you will find subjects relating to all aspects of life, from nature's seasonal struggles to the myriad of human emotions. Also included are poems about historical world affairs and every day events that give us pleasure and also annoy us. A good cross section of life filled with its vivid variety.

Some poems will amuse, others are sensitive or factual, drawn from personal experiences and observations, and also facts in life. Poems to entertain, uplift, learn by, and words to touch the heart and soul. We all have a story to tell and you may identify with the writer. These poems are written in many diverse rhyming formats, many refrains created by the author. All written during 2022 and 2023. The majority of unusual formats have been identified at the bottom of each page.

Life leaves its scar on our heart, and rocks our spirit. We all leave our footprint behind no matter how insignificant we think it is, we are all making history in our own back yard. In all cultures, emotions are universally recognised, no matter who we are, we all have the same basic feelings. We are individuals with opinions. To be human is to err. We make a difference, even when we stumble.

Poetry not only records life, it identifies situations we face from a personal point of view that many of us can identify with and understand. Poetry makes us feel less alone as we are in this life together and face the same, or similar challenges every day. Rhyming words are powerful and can soothe the soul, lift the spirit, excite and infuse the reader with confidence and self-esteem. We hope to greet the sun every day with positivity, and if we keep love in our hearts, keep our faith, and believe in human nature, we will live a good life. Hopefully these words reach inside your soul and touch your heart within, sing to you, and leave a lasting word to ponder.

Enjoy: Poetic Reflections

Contents

A Burial

The sky was mourning with the rain as showers fell that day,
and wearing black we gathered at the graveside early May.
This precious soul in heaven now, goodbyes were hard for all,
no longer would he text a word, and never would he call.

A solemn serenade was heard reminding us of days
when he would joke and play the fool, we loved his carefree ways.
Alas the time had come, his life was laid into the ground,
and in the well-attended church, we never heard a sound.

And only when we heard a favourite song he always played—
did tears begin to fall and ardent sorrow was displayed.
We celebrated, swinging from our laughter to our tears,
a tribute paid to this dear man who gave us special years.

Dedicated to Kenneth Burrows who died 7th April 2010

A Caring Soul

Since we first met, I have thought much of you,
the helpful deeds and caring way you speak;
a mentor, as you teach your sweet technique,
you were the kindest man I ever knew.

Those helping hands for those who might be weak,
with honesty, integrity, are true;
your helpful deeds and caring way you speak,
that makes you who you are, and my love grew,
the perfect man for me, you are unique.

And when we dance, 'tis always cheek to cheek,
my heart is yours, together stick like glue—
your helpful deeds and caring way you speak,
a mentor, as you teach your sweet technique.

(An English Madrigal)

A Fresh Pair of Eyes

If only we had eyes that had a fresh unsullied look,
a spare pair we could use on dull, and cloudy, rainy days;
a view that is unprejudiced, an open hearted book—
our world is just a myriad of vibrant keen displays

A pair of eyes belonging to another can renew—
they spot mistakes, are curious, inquisitive their eye;
we hope that we perfect our words, but sometimes our debut
may not conform to grammar rules, and rhymes may not comply.

Allow another in, and let them read your precious work,
critique can be an asset overall, can change your view;
bugs are ironed out and errors fixed before they lurk,
if only eyes could freshen up and feel like they are new.

A Handmaids Tale

I see a pattern forming and it could be dangerous
control of legislation is becoming quite obsessed;
as women's rights are nullified with growing strong concerns,
fanatics have a deathly yearn, this attitude disturbs.

Restraint of individuals, and the threats against the crowd,
the prejudice against the female form is getting loud;
I fear that very soon a woman can't decide to wear
a skirt too short, her lips too red, or how they style her hair.

The narrow minded men who have the privilege of gender,
are poking in their noses, and the women will remember—
a time when witches drowned or perished at a burning stake,
they're targeting with laws so that they have no real escape.

A Life Wasted

A snap decision changed his life, he knew the consequences—
he'd made mistakes that caused him strife, he'd failed, with no
successes;
repeatedly he ran away— whenever life was tough,
he couldn't face what he' become, as life was built on bluff.

Bravado cheer, embellished truths, where weak foundations fell,
his sleepless nights, his conscience blights, it was a living hell.
And never once did he reveal, his heart was cold as stone,
he never felt compassion, as he had no love to own.

Alone without someone to love, he died inside a frost,
his eyes were cold, when he was old, he paid a heavy cost.
The joy of life, the simple things, were missed, he did not see—
how being loved and giving would have set his spirit free.

Now looking back the track is dusty, overgrown with weeds,
the planting season came and went, and wasted were those seeds.
It's all too late to contemplate, his history was dark;
a littered past of broken-hearts that lit an angry spark.

A Message to my Father

I fought against the rolling tide and stubbornly rebelled,
when met with such commanding words, I cried out and I yelled;
as I was just little girl, when I left my home for good,
to make a life without the man whom I misunderstood.
When he was young his Mother beat him with a boiler stick,
with no compassion, all alone, her lessons taught him quick;
but he grew anxious to escape and joined the ranks at sea,
he met and married his true love, at twenty they had me.

The discipline was strong and cold, his violence was real,
he threatened, and his word was bold and there was no appeal;
my sister was outspoken and his hand would hit her hard,
I kept my thoughts within my soul, would not let down my guard.
My Father, a misguided man who lost his way in life,
yet he would think he did his best, he always loved his wife!
But every child would battle with their childhood after that,
this dying man, now near his grave, did not know how to act.

But I am grateful for some lessons, I learned in my youth,
to Sunday school where I was sent, I learned from God, the truth;
I also learned that standing firm meant I could gain more strength,
and when I had my kids, I learned to compromise, relent.
I gave my children all the love, that I had missed when young,
I taught them to become good girls, and always use their tongue
to say the words "I love you" and to gently kiss at night,
and life is not about the struggle always to be right.

I think back to my Father's death when he refused to go,
I'm saddened that he missed out on my thoughts and what I know;
that I forgive him for my childhood days when I was sad,
and how I felt about him, as he always made me mad.
And I regret the fact that I deprived him of my truth,
my inner thoughts, my happy life, in contrast to my youth;
but maybe he would not believe in words I had to say,
but if he is still listening, I send my love today.

A Mighty Wind

The windy gust would not rescind
it pinned me to the wall;
the blooms were trimmed, as petals thinned,
the stems no longer tall.

The falling trees, as I recall
had all been torn apart;
the birds would stall, as they were small
and staying put was smart.

Remarkably the car would start
departing for the sky!
The horse and cart would also chart—
we thought we all might die!

We tried to bolt the shutters tight,
and tied them with some rope;
the roof took flight, and like a kite,
it left us with no hope.

Winds hit ay 6mph in Southampton, England, and took the roof off a house.
(A Metrical Echo)

A Misty Apparition

The mist, it lingers in the valley—
ghosts that never die.
A kiss of atmospheric folly,
tantalised the eye.

A shadow held suspended
in a fickle apparition;
it's menacing and splendid—
like an ancient superstition.

The condensation shrouds the scene,
the valley drowns in sorrow—
as mountains dream of Halloween
a scare they try to borrow.

The sun will dry the atmosphere
to leave a clearer view,
the silent mist will disappear
and steal the morning dew.

The eerie morn has shed its fright,
as sunlight warms the ground,
until the mist persists at night
when hazy vapours hound.

A New PM

A new PM for Britain here,
it's clear he's blue right through;
another crew will start to steer
I fear the changes too—

the taxes will now soar up high,
and pensioners will sigh and cry!

We need stability to reign
a change is guaranteed;
to stop the leaking wounds and pain,
contain and stem the bleed.

(A Pinned Decimal)

A Pitiful Life

The face presented to the world is one of happiness—
but when at home, the cold uncaring hand of his caress,
will often carry torment as there is a price to pay—
for living with a moody soul whose actions speak, not say.

And no one knows the debt accumulated over years,
the sorrow and the heartache that has brought so many tears;
and still there is no respite from the horror in his mind,
as those who know him well will know how he can be unkind.

I'm looking back remembering the details of a life,
that caused the painful suffering of many souls in strife;
and all alone he wallows in the pity of his state—
how everyone's uncaring, how he blames them for his fate.

A Poet's Mission

The morning fills with perfect peace before the cock awakes,
when everyone is fast asleep and my muse starts to rake—
as gathered are my memories that turn into a song,
and filtered are events, as I divide the right from wrong.

My thoughts on war and peace when my emotion boils my blood,
if only I had power to infuse the world with good;
alas I am a cog within the mighty wheel of life,
a poet with a feeble pen that wobbles with its strife.

Then suddenly a mighty sword is thrust into my hand,
I rule the world with words I write, and others understand;
that one soul to another can reach inside a heart,
and beat a drum so loud that they appreciate the art.

As messages in rhyme can ruffle feathers, tickle toes,
bring peace to troubled minds when lies and truth can be exposed.

A Quota Of Limericks

When writing your Limerick story,
remember to give it some glory—
as metre is keen
the melody lean—
with tales that are ever so naughty.

A lewd little touch makes it spicy,
with something that is rather dicey—
a hand up the skirt,
or dishing the dirt,
to lust up your Limerick nicely.

Ignoring melodious ruling,
your Limerick loses its schooling,
as syllable count—
will stop all the doubt,
your words will be very consuming.

Perfect all your lines in good metre,
as Limericks sound so much neater,
when adding a dash—
of smutty old trash,
and a dominant metre is sweeter.

(A Limerick)

A Selfish Child

The self-indulgent mind of youth
will never see the blatant truth,
when caught inside defiant traits,
one sided are these dull debates.

Confusion numbs, and mist will blind,
a selfish non-compliant mind;
entitlement will rule the day,
a tantrum is what's on display.

But if the truth is really known,
this child thinks they sit on a throne
and all around are there to serve,
and they should get what they deserve.

But soon they realise how cold
the world outside can beat and scold,
alone among a pack of wolves—
their pride and selfishness dissolves.

A Sombre Day

A sombre day with tears of sorrow
ends a life with no tomorrow;
remembering a life well lived
where mourners have so much to give.

We say goodbye and bless our Queen
this truly is a sombre scene;
respectfully I bow my head,
as sadness in my heart has spread.

She leaves behind a legacy,
a reign of true integrity;
she lies with Royal crowns of old,
her rule was fair and never cold.

I hear the voices of the choir
her majesty did not retire
fulfilled her duty to the end
my love and admiration send.

A Spoilt Child

The arrogance within the child
a wild insulting sham—
their word can trample on a smile
defiled by this sweet lamb.

A spoilt brat with bitter tongue—
forgive them all, because they're young.

An exercise in good respect
complexities will test—
and soon success will take effect.
Now vexed? Time to reflect.

(A Pinned Decimal)

A Visit from Mary

From skies she floats, umbrella-up
her magic starts to quell the din;
in nanny garb as black as soot.
she soon begins to stir and spin.

She will insist you pay attention,
there is so much that we can learn;
but first, dispenses with convention
her flippant banter can be stern

The principles are true and keen,
she's organised and brings a smile;
you won't believe what you've just seen
fantastical, her unique style.

Her carpet bag is infamous
her treasured curiosities
appear with a such a skilfulness
a cheery mix of oddities.

Her vain and poignant confidence,
and cheery disposition frees—
and leaves you with your providence—
as she imparts her expertise.

When Mary Pops into your life,
she steers you to the magical;
the sparkle that will kill all strife,
and she's just being practical.

A Woman Scorned

She was betrayed, but still dismayed by others who would back
the kind of thoughtlessness that sided with a mean attack;
as though the woman much deserved the treatment she received,
without the empathy that's given to the one deceived.

As if it was the woman's fault, her wifely duties short,
control had neutralised her heart, her patience overwrought.
Dictatorship within the home had silenced every tongue,
and good intentions on her part would be perceived as wrong.

Although her love had died, her loyalty had still remained--
until the final insult had completely drained and maimed.
And when she saw the light, it shone so brightly that it blinded,
the truth revealed behaviour that was harsh and bloody-minded.

Her keen retaliation was then seen as mean, vindictive,
the suffering for many years was finely tuned, perfected;
and bitterness can rise inside until the anger shows,
then suddenly the perpetrator cries from heavy blows.

If you're prepared to use abuse to manipulate another,
expect revenge to hail upon you, suffocate and smother;
as victims of abuse who stand their ground and stop the rot,
are heroes who fought back against assaults that would not stop.

Acceptance

Death may be the end of life,
but not the end of memories,
strength within may hold the strife,
and score inside our histories.

Legacies prolong our years
and guide our future family,
tragedies we grin and bear
can knit two souls uncannily.

Pictures from scenes long ago—
unwind our inner thoughts and prayers,
teaches through the hail and snow—
that all of us are climbing stairs.

(A Rimaric)

Acrid Rumours

The people love a scandal when
a name's dragged through the dirt,
with whispers of a horrid deed,
when someone has been hurt;
the zealous mob is misinformed,
and lies begin to fly,
before we know it, dirt is thrown,
and lands inside the eye!

Beware those jealous rumours when
they have no real foundation;
nothing started off this fight,
expect some desperation.
To keep a level headed stance,
we need to be pragmatic,
as stirring pots can be a sin,
and just a tad traumatic.

Remember Shakespeare's witches as
their cauldron boiled with snails;
encouraged was Macbeth as he
would listen to their tales.
The blood was on the hands of those
who murdered through their greed,
a rumour starts when planted is
an evil wicked seed.

So measure all opinions with
an open hearted gift,
or we'll be blinded by a scandal,
someone else is miffed;
and when we light that flaming candle—
rumours are released,
our judgement could be very wrong,
and there will be no peace.

Adventures away from Home

I've witnessed perfect sunsets from the mountain tops on high,
and held hands on the beaches as I waved the sun goodbye;
I've felt the chill of winter in a foreign land where snow
is very deep and smooths the slopes to ski from high to low.

I've rode the seven seas and made some friends along the way,
and photographed the wonders of the world here on display;
and captured is a life so keen to join in escapades—
recording joyful vistas that our nature still parades.

Returning back to walk upon the turf where I was born-
embracing close connections to my roots, I am foresworn;
adventures are okay as long as we still find a home
that's warm and filled with love and peace we have a right to own.

After the Battle

The silent smite, the aftermath,
a steaming rise, a warring wrath—
where bodies lay in bloody mud
are severed with a mighty thud.
The torn and tattered atmosphere,
left chilling memories so clear;
as every life once bright and new
is fallen sinew, mortal stew.

The disregard for human life
is evident within this strife,
there is no skill or heroism,
lucky breaks— just barbarism.
The men who wear their medals proud
are tortured by tormented cloud,
the battle scars that root within
are never cleaned of certain sin.

Do Politicians stop to think?
As war, it teeters on the brink—
until it lets the violence
spill blood upon the violets.
The mourning grief that follows war,
it gnaws away inside the core;
there is no cure for loss like this—
no remedy, no goodnight kiss.

Against the Clock

A minute poem I must write
I'll be contrite
as I confess
I'm in a mess.

As sixty seconds is too short
they call it sport—
to dash some lines
in fine designs.

So here it is my poem's done,
now I must run,
I have a date—
no time to waste.

(A Minute Poem)

Against the Odds

Against the odds he fought, he jumped through hurdles to achieve,
escaped the enemy and dodged the bullet, told the tale;
as giving in was something he could never have believed,
when justice, liberty and freedom needed to prevail.

A revolution full of heartbreak, passion and reform,
resilience and dignity begin to reign and win;
but can a man decide to change, survive a mighty storm?
To redesign his former self and disregard his sin.

The line is drawn, when good and evil closely come to blows—
a blurring, where the Devil and the Saint are touched inside—
compassion and true empathy, infused with "yes" and "no's"
and human nature sheds a tear for those who are denied.

The courage and the bravery of one who fights the fight,
against the odds he fought, he jumped through hurdles to achieve,
and is there such a man with history whiter than white—
as giving in was something he could never have believed.

Les Misérables is a show about courage, love, heartbreak, passion, and the resilience of the human spirit—themes which undoubtedly transcend time and place. Perhaps the most relevant themes, however, are related to the dignity of the human psyche.

Ageing with Spirit

Like ag'ed wine, maturing just gets better,
our understanding deepens with a chime;
and like the taste of good old English cheddar
our wisdom has developed over time.

There's something to be said 'bout living long,
it carries with it instincts of survival;
as we are never phased by something strong
we break it down, not let our troubles spiral.

We may not like the signs of ageing wrinkles,
attacks upon our bones from deep inside,
but whilst our brain still functions and it tingles,
we make our mark, continue on our ride . . .

whilst we're still breathing life inside our lungs,
accumulating years won't silence tongues.

(A Sonnet)

Ageless Words

My age is etched upon my skin,
although I am still young within;
I cannot hide advancing years
my many scars are souvenirs.

And looking back at yesterday
when life was busy, everyday;
my memories are precious here,
as life has been so very dear.

How cruel it is to grow so old,
appearances that feel so cold;
when deep inside a fire burns,
dismissed am I by connoisseurs.

But when my pen inks with my words,
I'm ageless, as my meaning irks;
as young and old are moved to tears—
and hidden are advancing years.

Air Raid Shelter

We played inside the shelter, even though there were no bombs,
my Grandma told her tales of how she feared for all the swans,
when Gerry dropped torpedoes over Coventry that night,
she prayed for war to stop, and put an end to every fight.

We listened to her stories, how she made a cup of tea,
and with her Primus all prepared she had a guarantee
that no one would go hungry and that no one would be cold,
with blankets and some sandwiches her story was foretold.

The war is over now, although the shelter still remained
and me and my young sister would just listen to the rain;
inside the air raid shelter we were cosy, it was fun,
reality was diff'rent for my Gran, she'd want to run.

Allan Pinkerton — Private Eye

Now Allan was a private eye,
he wasn't shy, but bold;
a stubborn man, and shameless too
he had but one pure goal—

to find the traitor in the camp,
the modus operandi here
to find the spy inside the house,
his actions now were clear.

This abolitionist of slaves,
would root for truth within—
he didn't have to look too far
to find the one with sin.

At parties officers let slip
their plans among their friends;
and too much drink would loosen lips
a charm offensive lends.

But Pinkerton was on the case,
no job was too big here,
he infiltrated, heard it all,
determined buccaneer.

A socialite called Rose was keen
to pass on secrets clues,
arrested and was tried in court
confederates would lose.

And when she was released, she fled
to Southern States she went;
to carry on her treachery,

for freedoms she'd prevent.

Allan Pinkerton was a Detective hired by Abraham Lincoln to find the spy who was passing on secrets to the Confederates during the American Civil War. The culprit was Rose O'Neil Greenhow, a supporter of the Slave Trade and Socialite who entertained the Union Officers, plied them with drink to loosen their lips and they revealed their secret plans of attack, dates and strategies.

Alpha Oscar One

Alpha Oscar One
eyes the target from the sky—
arresting success

Always the Bridesmaid, never the Bride

She danced like an angel and purred like a cat,
was always well dressed in her red feathered hat;
her pale sky-blue eyes and her silky blonde hair
would turn every head as they wanted to stare.

Her suitors were many, but none of them tried--
her beauty was unmatched by many a bride.
A princess, a fairy-tale prince would engage,
but no one attempted to ever upstage.

The flowering bloom would soon wither and die,
always a bridesmaid and never the bride--
put up on a pedestal, wasted, a sin,
perfection attained, but so lonely within.

Amazing Grace

He found redemption in the Lord
his deeds were unforgivable;
devotion truly forged reward
forgiveness now conceivable . . .
his prayers were answered on that day,
and he believed there was a God;
and rearranged his life to pay
a penance for his iron rod . . .
and so the song was born to all
his words ring true in life today—
as our beliefs prevent a fall,
our faith supports us on our way.

The story behind the song: "Amazing Grace"

Written in 1772, the words to the song "Amazing Grace" were penned from the heart and mind of John Newton. He was a slave trader and on one of his journeys he believed his prayers saved him.

He had a troubled childhood as his mother died when he was six years old. Newton spent years as a servant slave trader and on a return voyage to England, a storm almost sank the ship and he cried out to God to save them all. Newton later became a professional slave trader himself and admitted to treating the salves badly. He eventually devoted his life to the service of God and became a priest in the Anglican church, he subsequently penned 280 hymns and one of them was "Amazing Grace".

An English Soldier

An English soldier's kit bag would consist of basic stuff,
a towel, soap and shaving dish, some powder for his foot;
an extra pair of woolly socks, a canteen flask and cup,
a bacon tin and condiments when things were looking up.

A soldier's life was hard and cold, in trenches war controlled,
the narrow ditches, wet latrines, that often overflowed;
conditions meant that some would die, before they saw some action,
pneumonia would take a hold, and caused a chain reaction.

With bread and jam and boiled plum pud, and bellies full of tea,
their cream long johns and khaki wools were full of lice you see;
a soldiers life in World War One was desperately rotten,
and mostly those who fought this war, are sadly now forgotten.

An Englishman's Home is his Castle

The mystery inside a home can hide a life of joy,
a place where we renew, and self-esteem we redeploy;
and once the door's securely closed, there's privacy within,
a home is where the Englishman can dwell away from sin.

A world where only chosen ones are welcomed past the door,
and when you enter, due regard's expected, underscored.
A mutual respect, an oath to take off both your shoes—
obeying all the household rules, you never can refuse!

The castle is a sanctuary, strangers have no clout,
and every Englishman will have the right to throw you out!
Remember, even humble homes are full of inner pride—
and no one is entitled to defraud or steal or chide.

And all unwanted visitors will not be welcomed guests,
and calling unannounced denies your right to all requests.
The home's on sacred ground, it is a private place to play,
when in the homes of Englishmen, don't ever overstay.

An Ideal World

I took a trip around the world,
and witnessed lots of things,
I know that we can't fly about
without a set of wings;
with much determination
I uncovered truthful scenes—
and realised that everyone,
is looking for their dreams.

Inside the jungle forest,
on the streets of spry LA,
where every soul is looking
for a life with bold ballet,
a peaceful warm existence
where no evil can exist,
where everything is happy
and there is no fog or mist.

A Shangri-La, an ideal world,
where there's enough to eat;
a place where everybody has
a chance to be complete;
when I returned back to my home,
and slept all through the night,
it dawned on me that humankind
has need in life to fight.

Another Year has Just Slipped By

Anticipating twenty-three,
another year for you and me;
and looking back at all that cheer,
I have enjoyed throughout this year.
The spring when flowers fought the cold
and bloomed in pink and green and gold;
the eagles nested, hope was sworn,
that eggs would hatch, new life was born.

The smiles returned to faces too
as warmer climes helped us renew,
the summer won when everyone
enjoyed a picnic, bathed in sun.
Too soon the Autumn shed its leaves
reluctant trees had felt the breeze;
as preparations had begun
for winter's cool and frosty run.

I feel a little older now,
a year that quickly passed somehow;
my memories are fixed when I
remember time has just slipped by.
I'll celebrate the ups and downs,
and welcome next year's sights and sounds;
be thankful that we all survived,
as life was joyful, we have thrived.

Happy New Year 2023

Anticipation of Trouble

Uneasiness has filtered through,
as I can sense a change in you.
I used to hear the sound of love
romantic song with hope above—
but lately there's a diff'rent tune,
as troubled thoughts begin to loom.
A shadow follows me around—
a cloud of dread that seems profound.

Should I ignore the moment here
that's lacking in a happy cheer?
Or should I ask if something's wrong
and hear the truth, when I'm not strong.
My heart is saddened by the mood,
as if I'm guilty, I conclude—
I'll wait to see if trouble comes,
prepare myself for beating drums.

Appearances

She tries to prove she's different, to earn her place in life,
and dyes her hair, she's adamant to rise above the strife;
she hates to be invisible, she stands out from the crowd,
her actions are dismissible, behaving far too proud.

And when she goes to church her hats are always talked about,
her avid online search has brought a style that is devout;
and when she passes windows, her reflection is admired—
appearances are everything for her to be desired.

But what she does not realise, her heart is what they see,
the hats may symbolise a spirit that is never free—
it matters not the way we look, what matters are the sparks
inside our eyes, that cheeky grin, the smiles within our hearts.

Arcade Games

The hum, the heat the numbing beat,
the arcade where the money cheats—
the deadening of senses— strong,
where bright machines play all day long.

Attracting kids to win, achieve
when all the time, machines deceive,
with hope to make a penny earn
and fill up pockets with return . . .

with every win the urge to try
to make an easy pay out high,
but games are set to keep your dosh,
they swallow money in their slots.

So how can playing slots be fun?
When leaving with a face that's glum,
there are no winners in this place—
the gamble is a big disgrace.

The bright Arcade attracts the kids,
for fun and games machines with bids
to draw a crowd, they sing out loud
and wasting money is allowed.

The odds are stacked against the win,
and with these games, they draw you in,
the habit forms in early age,
and innocently they engage.

Arcade games aimed at kids is big business. These places encourage kids to part with their money with the promise of a win and of course the odds of winning are stacked against them. The result is that they end up chasing the win until they lose all their money. This practice turns into a habit in adulthood. There should be a law against allowing children into these places.

Awkward Child

The awkward child did not fit in,
his actions seemed to be a sin;
the lack of understanding here
would change his life, it would appear.

In ignorance they left him there
abandoned in a home of care;
as neither of them had the guts
to sacrifice, too many buts.

And others saw the light within,
and taught the child to star and win;
he prospered with a caring hand
and learned to lead his own command.

Now grown he knows who he believes
the truth is that he is relieved—
and thanks to souls who gave him love
so that he grew and rose above . . .

and now his parents want their child
but it's too late to be beguiled;
his strong veneer is set in stone,
his love for them they'd never own.

Baby It's Cold Outside

I see you looking straight at me,
my feathers new, my feet are wee,
I'm learning from my ma and pa—
they tell me I will be a star.
Just now I think its cold outside,
I wear my overcoat with pride;
when I grow up and spread my wing
the scene will be fit for a King.

But I have lessons still to learn,
my eyes are wide, my ears still burn,
for everyone is watching me
my feathers new, my feet are wee.
When I perform my peacock show
how patiently the crowd will know—
displays will be for love's crusade,
delightfully I shall parade.

Back to Work

Now cranking up the old machine
to work again today;
it's tough, as everyone is still
in party mood and gay.
And work is just the last thing on
my mind, I'm on a cloud,
and then I hear the horn, my train,
is brutishly too loud.

I board and sit among those
dedicated to the grind,
my heart is still at home and I
just want my bed, unwind.
But here I am inside a tube
of metal set for hell--
the ride to work is arduous,
I'm under its great spell!

Battle on the Bus

The rickety old bus is coming down,
to take the workers, shoppers into town;
the seats are scarce, inside it heaves with people,
the passengers on board are far from gleeful!

The lower castes, they battle for a crust—
to earn a rupee, transport is a must!
These villagers who live a frugal life—
will ride the bus despite the crowded strife.

They hang onto the bumpers and the roof,
to ride this dusty road they know the truth,
contentment is rewarding in the bush—
but not without the battle in the bus!

Be Careful Who you Trust

Remain steadfast in your beliefs, and never sway from truth,
foundations built on facts, not brief encounters from our youth.
Uncovering a lie reveals that not all men are honest,
the revelation seals our fate, we learn to act upon it.

The treachery is strewn along the paths we walk in life,
our ears are filled with strong opinionated men with strife;
and my advice is filter, listen hard to make a choice,
I empathise, console those who are silenced with no voice.

Be careful what you wish for as our wishes can come true,
and concentrate integrity on knowing who is who;
manipulators, liars are out there to suck us in,
beware, and only trust those who keep honesty within.

Be in Control of your Life

Dismissive and indifferent, I feel the pain of it,
although I know I need to keep the faith, I will admit
that this manipulation should not coax me to conform,
I have the right to live my life, without a mighty storm.

My choices have to be my own, and being free is key,
I cannot live my life without it being about me;
so I will write, and I'll continue with my words and views,
not be coerced by others, as I have the right to choose.

The undermining comments and the numbing attitude,
is tantamount to cruelty and it disturbs my mood;
but I will rise above this din and make my way in life,
and never let this interruption bring about some strife.

I'm riding on a wave so high, that I can feel the breeze,
It's flowing through my hair and I enjoy its soothing ease;
I know I am not perfect, but I also know I'm keen--
to make the most of life, create my own unique routine.

Behind the Veil

He hid behind a veil of silence
nothing would be said;
for selfishness he had a licence,
conscience never led.

And lack of empathy had driven
into thoughts on gain;
remained one of those unforgiven
men who lived with pain.

The odds were stacked against his freedom
shackled by his greed;
a tree within the arboretum—
rot was guaranteed.

Bending Nature

The laws of nature have their flaws
and doors are sometimes closed;
to reach the shores without our oars,
unguarded, we're exposed.

Proposed alternatives may flow,
when chosen by ourselves;
as we impose and we disclose—
our stubbornness rebels.

We tell a tale, and use our spells
to quell the angst and strife,
as changes sell, ideas dwell—
on making good our life.

(A Metrical Echo)

Betrayed Forever

My eye betrayed by scenes I can't forget,
as actions speaking volumes tell a tale;
the facts confirm deep feelings of regret
when vindication has the will to fail.

The spiteful deed was meant to cut like blades
and bleed with its undoing of all trust;
now all that's left are wild words in tirades
that resonate in history— combust.
Now looking back as time has changed our future,
I realise that I cannot forgive;
some deeds are just too evil for a suture
when wounds remain so raw that they still live.

Occasionally I will think of you—
upon my soul you left a dark tattoo.

(A sonnet)

Beware: The Candy Smile

I hear a sweet and touching word—
behind it there is treachery;
for spite can chill when cheaply stirred,
a hateful documentary.

Betrayed is trust when turned to dust
all loyalty and kindness gone;
and when a word has been unjust,
the battle may have just begun.

Beware those with a candy smile,
behind it is duplicity;
for deep within they are hostile,
no ounce of authenticity.

Birthday Cheer

Our birthdays mark the years
and count our memories within;
so dry all saddened tears,
and hear a tuneful violin.

The stars are bright and shine—
their sparkle sprinkles fairy dust,
as I have sent you mine,
and hope that some of them you touch.

I hope you find contentment,
wherever you may rest your head;
let go of all resentment,
and fill your life with love instead.

I send you cheer from here,
with hope today will soothe your soul;
and may your future steer
you on a path to keep you whole.

Blending Paint

An artist sees beyond the scene into the undergrowth,
and touches deep beneath the leaves to paint with soul— an oath;
to capture mood, bring life to movement sewn into the canvass,
with every stroke the brush is keen to learn from all that practice.

We look into the picture and we see through eyes of old,
the paint has dried, but what remains is warm and never cold;
success has been achieved when oily colour is applied,
when eyes of those who look can see the reasoning inside.

Like poetry, a painting can evoke and stir the heart,
and bring a tear of sadness that can tear the soul apart;
the images of nature or a battle field of death,
a single stroke of genius has the power to take breath.

Simplicity, complexity are words that can describe—
the different approaches to a scene to be designed.
The artist has the power to imprison every thought,
creating something magical where we have all been caught.

Blossoming Love

My love is like a fragile bloom—
revealed are hearts when open;
the petals here have lots of room
to mend a heart that's broken.

The stem is sturdy at the root,
with strength to ride the storm;
but if bad weather is acute,
the flowers here may mourn.

A constant wind will scatter heads,
in pieces they will die;
my love within is torn to shreds,
will never reach the sky.

But peaceful summer sunny days
encourage love to blossom;
in eager colourful displays—
aromas that smell awesome.

Boston Tea Party

Strong Indian leaf
taxed the minds of colonists
sips of hot tension

Bully Boys

When envy kills morality,
it frees a mean brutality,
we see another fall to fate,
when helping them is far too late.

Behind the scenes sad tears are shed
instead of joy, a rumour spreads,
and threads of sorrow start to burn,
deceitful words show no concern.

As brash impertinence hits down below with speed,
the plea for permanence we know is sown from greed.

The victim learns their talent soars
as war has caused those saboteurs
to pour the rain upon their flame,
to dull their shine and cause them pain.

(The Tetravalent)

Buried Memories of Old

Buried deep are memories of old
that burn our future with such damning cold—
snapping at our heels is history
indelible . . . . this stamp of misery.

Gnawing stories filled with bigotry,
injustice and corruption loose and free—
captive are the souls from yesterday,
we must remember all of them, and pray.

Chronicled in words by scholars here—
the facts we can't ignore, they are severe;
wars that bring the sorrow and the grief,
remembrances that steal just like a thief.

Calm + Tranquil

A whole new world was gifted here,
I welcomed it with greatest cheer;
I entered into ageing times,
that prompted many diff'rent rhymes.

An outlook and a slower pace,
still running with the human race;
adventure is within my bones,
and I will not succumb to moans.

The urgency of troubles now
will take a backseat, dim somehow;
I'll not be moved to rush about
when something happens with a clout.

I'll take my time, consider time
and not allow a heinous crime;
or stamp its feet in temper storms,
a calm persona in me forms.

The chaos of the world outside,
will not enter deep inside;
my meditation takes me to
a place where I remember you.

A soothing sea and sandy beach
where the sun's within my reach,
and every time I view the blooms,
my senses smell those sweet perfumes.

Cassowary Tales

He darts about like he's on speed,
indeed he had some gall;
he never stalls, he's in the lead,
and he can grow quite tall.
This Cassowary's full of fun
inquisitive
he's primitive
and loves to give
I visited
relived old times when he would run.

The closest relative to the Cassowary is the emu, native to Australia. These birds probably had a common ancestor 25-30 million years ago as birds first appeared in the Jurassic period (about 150 million years ago). This bird looks prehistoric.

(The Chime Operandi)

Change

There's nothing worse than change when peace has settled on the sun;
disruption, chaos reigns when something tells our brain to run;
the stress, it penetrates into the blood and into bones,
the panic in our eyes as we see many falling stones.

Solutions are not visible when cloud consumes our skies,
we never see the sun or hear the birdsong when they rise;
and all we know is change will bring us harm, we cannot see
the way to battle forward when we're blind to this degree.

We cannot turn the clock, we know that yesterday has gone,
and changes mean we have another climb to overcome,
but once we can accept that changes always cross our path,
then we can guide and combat through the murky aftermath.

Charming Sunset

Concealed behind the cloud, the sun descends—
Harpooned by rays of orange, pink and gold;
Admiring eyes look skyward at the blend.
Remaining focused on the golden globe.
Manipulating colour as it goes
Intensifying deeply with its rays—
Naively falling downward as it glows
Gigantic ball of fire still ablaze.

Spectacularly demonstrates its power
Unforgiving as it says goodbye;
Nobody sees a sunset in a shower
Saffron shades turn grey, the sun is shy.
Elated am I when the sun is setting
Tantalising me with its abetting.

(An Acrostic and Sonnet)

Choice is Yours

Never let your choices fall
into another's hands—
keep the power of your call
protect it from command.
Reach inside your soul, believe
that you have every right,
calmly state, you will receive
your just desserts, tonight.

Christchurch Priory

This pretty town is welcoming
the parish church is strong—
the inner walls are beckoning
and filled with psalms and song.

And fortified with faithful stone
this robust fortress— bold;
is where the love and hope is shown
and never is it cold.

A tranquil place where every face
is smiling back at me;
and worshipping is full of grace
and all of it is free.

I walked on sacred ground a while
and felt a tingle here;
the atmosphere was versatile,
as seasons change each year.

This parish priory is prized,
by all who view her faith;
by God himself she was baptised,
and in her fame she bathes.

Christchurch been here in England for over 1300 years, from the first Saxon building to this glorious Priory Church we view today. Throughout the centuries, worshipping God, through Jesus Christ his Son and inspired by the Holy Spirit, has been at the very heart of Priory's life and has been encouraged by its service to the local congregation.

Seldom has the voice of praise been silenced within these walls: it happened during the reign of King John, when the country was under Papal censure; once, at least, as a result of the bubonic plague; and recently because of the coronavirus. Our prayer and worship continues, but in new ways through the internet at times. This Priory Church is open to visitors from around the world as well as for private prayer.

Cleaners

This poem's for the cleaners,
they move in overnight;
they pick up all the streamers,
that float about like kites;
the food that'd dripping down the cracks,
rotting smells impact
the fags, the beer, discarded wraps,
scenes here now distract.

And working hard are insects,
the animals and birds;
advantages of sucking up,
eating sweet desserts.
When dawn brings sunny prospects,
and empty is each street.
the sweeping may be complex—
the end result is neat.

I admire the cleaners
on the floor and in the air,
they sing, they chirp and buzz about,
to the earth they swear . . .
in cities and the countryside,
work is undertaken,
their rigour not misguided,
their loyalty unshaken.

Cold Eyes

A cold blank empty stare was there,
emotions that he couldn't share;
bewilderment had taken hold,
the feeling left me chilling cold.
I never read those inner thoughts,
outside I saw a person caught
in a place misunderstood—
our world had little chance to bud.

Perception was so difficult,
it seemed a solid wall was built,
and drowning on the other side,
was someone with a lot of pride.
I tried my best to reach beyond,
to touch his spirit, I was fond;
but all I felt was loneliness—
without connection, helplessness.

There was an innocent display—
that drew my heart to come and play;
a fragile temper burst my bubble,
all I got was double trouble.
And now when I reflect on things,
the situations had some stings;
I mostly learned about myself
resilience, my inner wealth.

I don't regret a single climb,
my love it stood the test of time;
and when I think about the past,
it all went by so very fast.
One thing stood out above all else,
it took a toll upon my health—
and life was never dull with you,
my heart, it wears a deep tattoo.

Come on Sloopy, Come on!

With One foot in the grave, this man, he is still hanging on,
as Sloopy's let his hair down and he's not about to run;
oh shake it, shake it, shake it baby, open city gates,
and let the immigrants come in, and let's all celebrate.

You weaponised the FBI, and parents were upset,
and cut defence, now wars around the world become a threat.
Extremist ideologies are now as bad as Cuba!
So hang on Sloopy, you may be unfaithful, just like Judah!

Your war on fossil power drove the prices through the roof,
and crime is on the increase, as the law thinks you're aloof.
Withdrawal from Afghanistan meant chaos has resumed.
What happened to the US Policy?   It's been entombed!

Now you are being tested, Israel is on the news—
negotiating peace will be a challenge to your views.
As turning once again away from conflict indicates—
your spineless back has been relaxed into a muted state.

The shameful list is growing with incompetence it seems—
but Sloopy you're just magical with left wing silly dreams.
So let go of your strangle hold and step down off your horse,
you've left the country dying, now it's time for a divorce.

Commonwealth Games in Brum

The silver and Gold,
the young and the old,
the running, the lifting,
stories unfold;
the tall and the short,
the sport on the court,
and born in my city,
I'm proud to report—

the games have begun,
let the athletes compete,
the bull takes the stage,
to greet and to meet;
in Birmingham where,
the culture is rife—
a place in my heart,
has just come to life!

The eyes of the world,
are focused right here,
we hope that the weather
stays bright and clear;
and welcomed are guests
with smiles on our faces;
my ancestry's steeped
inside all these places.

So fight for the medals,
go for the prize;
step on the podium,
spirits arise;
the best of the best,
be bright as a star,
the light from within,
will shine from afar.

Computers Rule

I'm learning from this great trustee,
in turn it learns from me!
I use a word repeatedly
and it won't disagree.

I teach myself a brand new skill—
it frowns at my slow steps;
but soon I skip along at will
and don't feel so inept.

Devices regulate our life
we have no choice today
and we will find ourselves in strife,
if we don't let them stay.

Computers rule the world you see,
we won't be free of them;
our need is great, they set us free
but sometimes we condemn.

Controlling Minds

Decisions made by other men
who pen with venom time again,
and when we make a stand in time
we never want to toe the line.

The bitterness at what they did,
a fib we just will not forgive;
amid the chaos and the strife,
we will protect and save our life.

And so revenge takes root within our heart and soul,
as history records the stories that are bold.

If we let go of anger here
will cheer replace and help us steer?
As clearly those who start a fight
will always think that they are right.

(The Tetravalent)

Corruption

The governor had fingers,
inside every baking pie,
corruption when it lingers,
has a chance to sting the eye;
the influence will flourish,
all around must be obeyed,
and every man he punished,
would be easily betrayed.

He climbed the social ladder,
and his wealth would follow suit,
as others didn't matter,
as his temper was acute;
he covered up dishonesty,
by bribing those in power,
and absent was all modesty,
when fraud began to flower.

He had the local sheriff,
deep inside his suit coat pocket,
he never paid a tariff,
'cos he always made a profit.
The town knew he was crooked,
and nobody cared that much,
corruption here was sugared,
with a dusty icing frost.

Courageous Blackbird and Me

Today a blackbird serenaded, knowing I was there;
I know how patiently he waited, so that he could share.
So I stopped in my tracks to listen, looking up at him,
his warbling song, his repetition, sounded like a hymn.

The moment I reached for my phone to video his show,
he flew away, I felt so wrong, to interrupt his flow.
A moment later there he was, he followed as I walked,
I sat upon a bench because, he wanted my support.

His tale of sorrow touched my heart, the song of his lost love,
how they were driven far apart by fateful wind above.
He spent his days in hopeful song that he would be united,
I told him that he must be strong, our courage was ignited.

The two of us alone, without our love to keep us warm,
he recognised me and my doubt, survivors we were sworn—
despite our fears, the tears we've shed, we'd both remain with cheer,
and so we two would smile instead, in song we persevere.

Covid Chant

The chain reaction in the main
began a raging major plague
that left a stain on all mankind
a murky, vague and horrid reign.

The mind, the soul, the heart defined,
by menaces that choked inside;
the breathless kind that takes a life,
to fight, we tried and were resigned.

It's rife, this airborne floating strife,
you cannot see or hear its voice;
it kills your wife, your son, your friend,
we have no choice but face the knife.

The trend will not come to an end,
as Covid seems to spread like fire
we can't pretend that it has gone,
it won't retire, we are condemned.

(The Cryptic Labyrinth)

Covid Testing

Like sheep we waited patiently,
in line, with masks in place;
a Covid test that recently
will leave its track and trace.

An inefficient service here,
they chatted over coffee,
and queues of people stood in fear,
among them, there was Dolly!

We're at the mercy of these buggers
raking in the money,
accumulating many coffers—
sheep don't think it's funny.

A rip off, that is what it is,
to make a dime, and run.
The Covid panic is a swizz—
and queuing is no fun.

Cracking Eggs

When breaking eggs, we crack the shell
and some may think this could be hell;
to make an omelette, eggs will quake,
as progress will not give or take.

The opposition could be strong
and many think that we are wrong;
but moving forward has to mean
accepting changes that are keen.

The moral of this little tale,
is never bulk or shout or wail;
or fight against what has to be—
as progressing will set us free.

Crime Goes Unpunished

It's not enough to witness crime
you have to prove it happened;
and no one seems to have the time
'cos no one is impassioned.

So those who threaten, instil fear,
can whisper words of hate;
when they are wholly insincere,
the terror won't abate.

It starts off small and escalates
and then there is a war,
the Police will not investigate
and violence will soar.

The minor crime is overlooked,
as busy men in blue
have schedules that are overbooked—
and so all crime just grew.

Crimes of Violence

Society believes in those who lie—
and truth can be disguised, some tongues are silent;
then quietly deceit will even try--
to hide behind the powerful and vi'lent.

The threat concealed, no proof means there's no crime,
and those who need protection won't survive;
the law will not believe you, they'll decline
and left are you to try and stay alive.

If someone stalks you, breaks into your home,
one word against another is no use,
you may be left defending on your own
and suffer the attack and the abuse.

And only when your death has been revealed,
will all the lies reported be repealed.

Shana Grace reported a former boyfriend (Michel Lane) for stalking her to the Police five times in six months. They interviewed him and he said he was still in a relationship with the woman and that she is making a fuss about nothing. The Police then fined the woman £90 for wasting Police time. The man then broke into her home and murdered her.
(A Sonnet)

Crusading for Peace

Our love should spread its wings when Christmas feeds
into our hearts with goodly deeds around;
each year we hope that peaceful word succeeds
in mending rifts, our bonding will be crowned.

I pray that compromise will win the day,
and showing mercy has its turn to shine;
where every man can see that it's okay
to live inside a world that's good and kind.

Alas the conflict terrorises cheer,
releasing with its venom, all the hate;
for victims filled with terrifying fear,
it seems that love and peace arrive too late.

Despite our diff'rences, we're all crusaders—
there's strength in learning how to live with neighbours.

(A Sonnet)

Crusading Nature

How blessed I am to see the dawn
and hear the chorus praise the light;
as night agrees to be withdrawn
and lets the sun rise up so bright.

How blessed I am to see sun set
and close my eyes when darkness falls
the white moon lets the silhouette
of boughs beleaguered to ascend.

But I know I am blessed to see
the summer, fall and winter too—
as spring will change in front of me
this season's glory will renew.

And life is eager to enjoy—

from dawn 'till dusk, from light to shade—

as change is constant, it will toy
and tease us with its fine crusade.

Curry Night

As love was in the fine detail,
and detailed in my dreams
are all the times you never failed
to bring us great cuisine.

Your expertise in artful food,
you wowed us with your curry;
and served with saffron rice— the mood
fantastical and funny.

The Chana Dhal, a spicy treat,
remembering those days;
and I recall those tasty eats—
the smell of herb bouquets.

I miss you in the kitchen here,
enthusiastic cheer;
when you enjoyed a German beer
in heat you'd persevere!

My cooking skills are limited,
I need a skilful hand;
you left the earth inhibited
without you, nothing's planned.

Curse of the 21st Century

Inventions like the wheel, have changed our lives,
as human ingenuity is key—
but looking back at what has since transpired,
our lazy ways will never make us free!

The motor car has saved our legs from walking,
and so we've gained some weight we cannot shift—
computers mean from armchairs we are blogging,
so are these aids a joyous thankful gift?

Now chairs are motorised we will not move,
as we can get about without our legs—
how can this be a life that has improved?
When idle limbs give up! This question begs?

"Will evolution mean we cannot walk?
Will we be born without our lower limbs?
The more we reach for aids, the more we talk
of ways to never go for runs in gyms".

I'm seeing youths take to the mobile chair,
to get from A To B, they use a scooter!
As automation means we never care—
to ever walk, just sit at our computer.

I realise that those who are impaired,
will need the help of mobile chairs to move,
but able bodied folks should be aware,
that walking means their health will be improved.

Curse of the Uber-Eat Delivery Gang

Sometimes there's hustle bustle going on outside my door
these noisy folk care nothing for the silence I adore.
They gather in a group and shout and kick the ball about,
the neighbourhood would benefit if they were ousted out.

These are not kids, but adults who have nothing much to do,
they break the rules, they are such fools, their antics are taboo.
I have complained, but they remained, the mindless have no brains,
a car blares-out, loud pounding shouts, from music it contains.

And every Sunday morning I am woken by these men
who gather with their Uber bags delivering again;
the city with their fast food shops that sell a heart attack
to people who are lazy, as they carry too much fat!

The punks who make a bob or two from those who never cook,
like leaches they adhere to those who just don't give a "damn".
The slamming doors and squealing wheels, as tyres speed away,
my wish is that they don't return, as this is not okay.

Living in the city has its drawbacks as I am surrounded by fast food restaurants where Uber-eat delivering drivers gather waiting for early morning orders for breakfast. They park illegally and whilst they wait, they play ball, slam doors, shout and play loud music in their cars.

They don't live in my town and are there for the sole purpose of delivering fast food to those who are too idle to make their own breakfast! They are noisy, and once they have an order, they speed away like racing car drivers. It is annoying.

Damned Device

My screen is bright and lively when my mind should be asleep,
it beckons me to find thee, for my eyes will take a peep.
And even when I pull the plug, the images are there,
They're dancing in my head and bug me as they want to share.

No discipline will tear me from the magic of the screen,
it follows me and taunts you see, it can be really mean;
and when I shut it down at night, I hear it beep and ring,
it never lets me fly my kite, I'm tied to it with string.

And only when the battery has died, is there relief,
as I can take a break from it, although it will be brief;
as this device has stolen every bit of my free time,
I should report it to the Police as a heinous crime.

Dancing 'til Dawn

I wrapped my arms around his waist
we then embraced,
he kissed my face;
we danced
'till dawn
what fun
a rising sun
had just begun
a whirlwind was this new romance.

(The Novenary Reel)

Day After Christmas

'Twas the day after Christmas when all through the house,
not a person was stirring, not even the spouse.
The stockings were empty, the chimney looked bare,
and no one recalled if St Nick had been there.

The children were out at a neighbours for tea,
the scene, one of carnage— with lots of debris.
wine bottles were empty, beer cans everywhere,
a stranger was slumped on the lounge easy chair.

Then suddenly someone just fell out of bed,
and hit the floor hard with a bump on the head;
now dazed and cross-eyed and drunk from the wine,
he signalled to say that he would be just fine.

The kitchen where turkey was stuffed in at speed,
the carcass was rotting as cats tried to feed.
The tinsel was trailing all over the floor
and silk underwear was thrown over the door.

Was Christmas all worth it, the prep took so long,
the place is a mess, did we all get it wrong?
A boxing day clean means there's much work to do,
or the Mother-in-law won't be happy with you!

Dean Kouch gave us a Fright!

Of all those hearts I miss the most, with fondness I remember,
the horror writer Dean who was a poet and a member.
His chilling work still touches me, he wrote straight from the heart,
and often every word he wrote would tear my soul apart.

He ruffled feathers, dug down deep into the hearts of men,
producing many poems from his horror inking pen.
We miss you Dean as you may be a turning in your grave
and listening and reading all the poems of the brave.

You never wrote about the pain you suffered every day,
or moaned about your health, you were so generous and gay;
I miss your presence on this site, the humour in your posts,
and your reviews were welcomed by the members and the ghosts!

*This poem honours a poet called Dean Cook who died four years ago. He
wrote horror poetry and delighted us with his chilling stories and poems. He
is greatly missed.*

Death and Destruction

The stone cold hand of death
descends upon the city with a frosty chill,
leaving stone relics of a former life.

The fire burned and the lead flew—
ripping into flesh, spilling innocent blood.

Streets were left with a ghostly echo of what was once
a town with vibrant and lively prospects.

As the dust settles there is no regret
among terrorists who are enthused by destruction,
and the dawn just brings another day of hate.

This is WAR, and anything is possible,
crimes are committed in the name of victory.

The steely determination of one man in a quest
to kill, maim and torture another.

We see men working for the Devil
and the rest of the world watches in horror—
evidencing man's inhumanity to man.

And not until there is no opposition
will the noisy bombs cease to blow.

The city is conquered by avaricious greed
and self-interest of a blood-thirsty madman.

The reaper moves in to mop up the aftermath.

Death Dodgers

My mission is to dodge the Reaper when he comes to call,
he may think he has super powers— I will lock my door!
I notice that some older folk have lived beyond their years—
they've brought the reaper to his knees, as he is left in tears.

Success is in the stealthy way that we can dodge a death,
rebel, defy and don't comply to taking your last breath.
Resist the odds, survive and live a few more years beyond—
if death comes knocking at my door, I never will respond.

If you are getting on in life avoiding death is fate,
but I believe that if you fight then you can change the date;
so push yourself, go ride a bike, go walking in the park—
and you'll avoid the Reaper where his world is always dark.

So dance 'till dawn, and never yawn, play games before you're dead,
and don't give up when life is tough, as age is in your head;
go beat the clock, run round the block and keep your heart alive,
and this is my advice to all, ensuring you'll survive.

Deceit

A whisper, or a rumour, caught inside the ear
at first it is unclear until that realisation,
that moment when we know the hidden truth—
deceit that has broken our trust,
and shattered our heart.

And torn apart is all our love in this betrayal—
we have been misled, duped and outwitted.
Gathering our thoughts, our eyes are open,
and nothing will blind us now.

Sat in the park overlooking the lake
our thoughts wander into the past—
how pretty life was, how light-hearted
and tender were words—
how foolish we have been
     and now enlightened,
          we are scarred for life.

Deceit is Inherent

He feeds upon the dead, until the bones are bare,
and coldly leaves his mark that he was there;
the indiscretions of the past, he cannot share—
now turning to his faith, he didn't care.

Inherent is deceit, the cold and damning deed,
no matter how he prays, his sin will seed;
no humble thought, but menacing his manic greed,
to gain position, power to succeed.

Now resting on his laurels, he will not be judged,
he made amends, but truth is often fudged;
and only those within have rights to bear a grudge—
for they knew all the sorrow they have trudged.

Deep Regret

When in disgrace, my deed was unintended,
I weep alone, no one can understand--
the deep regret when someone is offended,
as hurt was caused by my own thoughtless hand.

The clock cannot reverse to change the deed,
all explanations seem so very weak;
repeating past events will serve to feed--
and taunt the action louder with critique.

My punishment is real, I mourn in silence,
forgiving not forthcoming in my mind;
self-loathing has been given lawful licence,
as I now know my action was unkind.

Although I think I'm innocent of crime,
regret belongs to me, it is all mine.

(A Sonnet)

Degradation of War

When war disrupts the basic laws, the suffering begins,
with little true humanity, there will be evil sins;
the vulnerable and the weak are prey to men with arms,
and facing someone in control will set off those alarms.

Brutality will rise just like an ugly Devil's head,
and leave a trail of blood and bones, a pit full of the dead;
and buried are the sins, until the nightmare ghouls appear,
as shadows of the past will threaten, as they persevere.

The lack of pity is instilled in those who go to war,
and feeds the mouths of lions as the conquering will roar;
it breeds a sense of cold indiff'rence for our fellow men,
remaining steadfast to the fight, to feed the war again.

Dehumanising humble souls, degrades their human status,
devaluing with degradation shows how people hate us.
Such persecution does exists and people are discarded,
and dignity, humility is often disregarded.

The aftermath will scar the minds and spirits held inside,
there are no winners in this fight, no honour and no pride;
the reasons why we go to war when humans can't agree—
is due to ego, fame and gain, to win and prove we're free.

Dependent on Drink

His stare would say it all, as mental thoughts were disengaged,
his brain was focused on the reasons why he was enraged;
the stupor numbed his face and stripped his normal good expression;
his veins polluted with the wine, to dull his deep depression.

Addiction started slowly with a tipple here and there,
his broken heart was in despair no words could even share;
sensations of euphoria would stop the heart from aching,
the whiskey bottle ruled his night, the dawn was full of shaking.

Neglectful of himself and others, all the care was gone,
a downward path of losing games had only just begun;
he did not see the morning light, just shadows in the dark,
the future years turned bleak, and they had lost desire and spark.

A winter robin chirping songs with melodies that soothed,
he watched the bird, was touched inside, uplifted was his mood;
it bobbed along the window-sill, was looking for a meal,
and soon outside he fed the bird, perhaps his heart will heal.

Determination

The inner urge to push on through
to do much more, ambitious too;
debut a talent, shine above,
addictive is this kind of love.

These strong, courageous fighting genes,
are seen as gallant traits in Queens;
between two rocks there is a bloom
determined to exude perfume.

Succeeding means that every thought should be applied,
and few will persevere to prove they own the ride.

But those, against all odds, will fly,
defy the facts to climb up high
untie those shackles, live the dream,
be resolute, without a team.

(The Tetravalent)

Devils at Work

Disciples of the Devil are at work in streets and lanes,
They're spreading propaganda in the hills and on the plains;
as everyone is listening when evil starts to grow,
and under stones and roots it starts to mushroom down below.

The hatred has a tendency to stew and come to boil,
malignant with its cancer it can fool and it can foil;
and everyone is woken, wicked words begin to sprawl,
and rioting and civil war manipulate, and maul.

The lies and cries of those who want to stir a troubled spoon,
unhappy with themselves, they even hate the stars and moon;
the gossips with a jealous rumour scatter fear around,
and you won't see it grow, as it all happens underground.

Disappointments Steal your Soul

It comes in many guises,
and it tends to steal our fun,
as disappointment will devour,
our soul when it is done;
we dwell upon the moment
and we analyse our time,
and wonder if we could have changed
the outcome of our climb.

If only this, if only that,
but in the end we know,
that we should just accept it,
and move on through heavy snow;
tomorrow is another day
and opportunity,
will knock again if we retain
some confidence and see . . . .

that sometimes fate can change our course,
we learn to stay awake,
and disappointment teaches to
avoid the same mistake;
a time to take a look at what
we want from life's sweet song,
reflecting on the past reminds,
that something might be wrong.

As discontent, and failure might
encourage us to see—
a diff'rent way to live our life—
with some sweet harmony.
If you are disappointed then
you may rethink your goal,
as chasing dreams you cannot reach
can stain your heart and soul.

Disillusioned Minds

With murder and with force, the ruling Kings and Queens would pay,
a revolution brought about a communistic way.
Reality is harsh and cruel, the poor remained in rags,
and still the regime failed to fix the problems and the snags.

Oppression leaves a heavy cloud that rests upon their head,
and keeps the people in a place of fear and social dread.
No freedom of the pen, or verbal exercise with words,
all thoughts suppressed, opinionated tongues are duly curbed.

The people have no right to know the secrets of the house,
and blinded they remain, cannot express mistrust or doubts.
No forward thinking by the population as a whole—
no star can shine because they live and work without a goal.

The Bolsheviks united in their wish to rule the world,
and disillusioned spies began their treason filled absurds.
The socialists today are moving more toward the left,
if we lose our democracy, we will be left bereft.

Diverse Hearts

When hearts are made of silky cloth
and sewn with golden thread,
the touch of love will grow within
and even when they're dead--
the love they leave will never stop,
it lives beneath the skin.

Some hearts are made of flimsy paper
substance then is lost;
we learn deceit betrays their soul
and heartache is the cost.
A lesson taught by every traitor
guarding with control.

And when a heart is made of gold
it's solid, firm and loyal--
reliability depends
on something that is joyful;
supportive are these hands to hold,
as flowing love transcends.

Do not Call on a Sunday

As Sunday is a day of rest,
a guest may come to call;
and it will test our nerves at best,
as interruptions stall.

Appalled are we that in the hall,
they called, we were not dressed!
We now forestall them, please don't bawl,
just leave us folks to nest.

At best I will deter requests—
suggest today's not good,
I may protest, as I am stressed.
"Not Sundays", "Understood?"

(A Metrical Echo)

Do Not Give Up when Challenged by Old Age

Do not give up when challenged by old age,
let not the light inside dim with the night;
another day will help you to engage.

The bravest souls live on, enjoy the stage,
continue with the lifelong inner fight
do not give up when challenged by old age.

And some stir souls with power and with rage,
take up their pens to paper, poems write;
another day will help you to engage.

So publish words to bounce upon the page,
use strength and courage, keep the future bright;
do not give up when challenged by old age.

Infuse with hope to turn that heavy page,
and push the boundaries, fly high your kite;
another day will help you to engage.

Go break the lock, don't stay inside your cage,
to touch and hear and smell, use sight, excite;
do not give up when challenged by old age,
another day will help you to engage.

(A Villanelle)

95

Do Not Want for More

Try not to want for more in life,
the yearn will surely bring you strife;
be satisfied, content with days,
for gratefulness will quell malaise.
Our needs are few, yet we want more,
achieving more can be a chore;
to strive for it, can take our money,
when life's already sweet as honey.

The greedy mind can sink our dreams,
as want and need are diff'rent things;
a lesson that we all must learn—
as greedy fingers cause concern.
Enough's enough, excess is stress,
and we can manage on much less;
be frugal, do not waste a penny—
when already you have plenty.

Dodging the Reaper

The little things we cannot do,
are signs of our demise;
our ever changing ageing view
means death is on the rise.

Our lazy attitude and mood
will knock another nail
into the box of gloomy doom,
confining us in jail.

The fight will soon be lost as we
submit to failing parts;
the hearing loss; eyes cannot see,
and broken stabbing hearts.

But fight we will until the last
to breathe in life is fun;
so buck the trend and have a blast
before we all succumb.

Dogs Know

Dogs don't care for looks or age
status, wealth or fashion trends;
freedom means they will engage,
every dog loves making friends.

Dogs know personality,
sniffing who you are inside;
souls reveal instinctively—
dogs will know if you have cried.

Dogs will know someone is mean,
senses tell them what is right;
cold and frozen hearts are seen
tales will wag at warmer sights.

Dogs love serving up their best,
unconditionally give—
loyalty and happiness
always ready to forgive.

Double Standards

The double standard of the law—
as from abortion they withdraw;
but they support the execution
deaths allowed by institution.

They play at God, do as they please,
electrocute, lethally freeze,
but when a foetus has a defect,
the law is not allowed to reject.

So why in this society
there is an absent piety?
Are people here devout and true?
Or are some changes overdue?

Is it okay to kill a man
and go against the bible's plan?
But where's the empathy for life?
The law's an ass without insight.

Can man decide who lives or dies?
Ignore the plight of women's cries?
And in despair the law takes hold,
and has a brutal hand that's cold.

Dreamy Memories

I never thought I'd leave this place,
cocooned in love and peace;
but wings were made to fly with grace
to find my soul's release.

So fly I did, and found new heights
I soared and found a guy—
who gave me everything, my flights
were blue, with cloudless sky.

Adventure came and went and now
I'm settled in my home;
I've flown around the world and vow
to never ever roam.

My memories are in my head,
and when I close my eyes;
I fly about when I'm in bed,
and praise each sunny rise.

Dressed to Weep

Waterfall leaves Spring
into cascading pleasure—
green petticoat tulle

Drunken Stupor

Respected by his peers, no tears were shed,
he had it all, a home, a car, a wife;
he felt the pressures heavy on his head,
and soon he felt the horrors of his strife.

He saw no sorrow in his glass of gin,
another calmed his mind, put him at rest;
and at the crack of dawn there was no sin,
he took the train to work to do his best.

Repeatedly this routine took its toll,
intoxication took away his words;
and lately spirit low, his life banal,
his drunken stupor brought him sweet returns.

He lost his job, his wife his home and car,
now on the street, and begging for a copper;
escaping from reality to star
in dreams where everything was good and proper.

He never saw the sorrow in his liquor—
for every drop took him to higher heights,
or thought the drinking was the very trigger,
now numb to all, including stressful nights.

The years were cruel, advanced by failing health,
there was no turning back, his life was doomed,
he never yearned for change or wanted wealth,
continued with the alcohol consumed.

His wife now places flowers on his grave,
at forty-six the bottle won the battle;
a lesson in addiction when we crave—
the boundaries are pushed, and soon unravel.

Eagles' White Hat

I yearn from birth to wear the white,
despite the grey, I learn;
when it's my turn to be a knight
I'll fight for my return.

I'll build a nest, and find a mate,
a hat of white, I just can't wait!

A wise and mighty Eagle be
you'll see me in the sky;
a fashion icon, you'll agree—
trustee of all I spy.

(A Pinned Decimal)

Early bird

The early bird
at 3 a.m.
The song I heard
was like Big Ben.

Awaking me
a twittering—
delightfully
delivering.

The sound of fun
for his true love,
before the sun
can shine above.

It's dark my dear,
so close your eyes;
though it is clear,
his heartfelt cries . . .

mean he can't wait
to send his word,
to make a date
this little bird—

keeps me awake!
Now I can't sleep,
song won't abate!
I'm counting sheep!

(Cube16)

Ego

When help is born from ego, it results in arrogance,
and manifests as bullying and leaves its evidence;
we recognise the self-assured conceit that is portrayed,
and preying on the weak is how oppressors ply their trade.

A smile delivers criticism— cutting deep inside—
insulting words of sarcasm are sneaky and they're snide;
denial is just part and parcel of these scheming souls
to elevate their status as a teacher who consoles.

The truth is that the only goal that ego has in mind—
to keep its self-importance at the forefront of design,
belittling those with talent so's to shine above the rest,
as ego thinks that it deserves to be the very best.

But never be a victim to the one who has an ego,
know that cowards deep within will never be a hero;
self-esteem is tempered by a humble, kind facade,
and ego has a tendency to leave a selfish card.

Ending Love

The night was young and stars were very bright,
indulgent was the radiant display;
excitement filled me with an ambient light;
I should have seen the signs that came my way.

I felt a nervous tension in the air,
the silence lingered after sun had gone,
and lack of conversation left despair,
as darkness fell too soon, the day was done—

and with it went my dreams, I shed a tear
for never would I see his face again,
the end had come, I felt a kind of fear,
unsteady was my walk, recalling when—

his words were few, as eyes spoke to my heart,
the bitter truth was out, and we would part.

(A Sonnet)

Ensign Wasp

His black flag waves above his back
with no intention to attack—
he hovers in the sunny light
this little guy will never fight.

His mission has a deadly trait,
he's patient, ready, lies in wait.
A brutish cockroach walks on by
not noticing this avid spy.

He lands upon his toughened wings
and to his body clings and stings
injecting eggs to hatch in time
and soon they eat from deep inside.

The cockroach slows as he's the host,
and doomed, he has been diagnosed.
This predator has warned from high
as his black flag has told us why.

*The Ensign Wasp is completely harmless to humans and pets; he has no
sting. He does however have a deadly mission for cockroaches as he lays his
eggs by injecting them into the insect and when they hatch they eat their way
out and the cockroach is doomed.*

Equal Rights for Women

If only those who grind their axe, could leave their angst at home,
show empathy for others, as so many are disowned;
the women who are left to fight, to bring up families,
without support, without the right to choose their fantasies.

Their prejudice and selfish ways will damn their future course,
those single minded guys who think they have a right to force;
and hiding in the wings their bias thwarts another's life,
shamefully they judge and think that their way has a right.

So blind to all the suffering, these souls who have no heart,
will see another torn and scorned, ensuring they impart
a sermon to the masses where they will believe in God
and yet unlike the Lord they have a grudge inside their blood.

Arise all those who want to fight for rights to always choose,
without the interference of those despots who abuse;
say equal rights for everyone, regardless of their sex,
discriminating minds should fear that their rights will be next.

Errors Missed

Our eyes may play a trick on us,
we trust to some degree;
we miss a word, and cuss,
as in plain sight, we do not see.

A misspelt verb, a spot of ink,
a link we should have seen;
a buckle or a kink--
a sign that something's in between.

Our brains are sometimes on the blink,
naively we are blind;
and so computers think
of errors we have left behind.

(The Octahex)

Eve of Christmas

Excitement mounts the day before
so many chores, still left to do;
the crew are waiting at the door,
the sleigh tonight makes its debut.

The reindeer line up for the ride
as Rudolf guides the team despite
the blight of hail and ice outside,
a chain of friendship brings the light.

The funny elves are buzzing round,
I hear the sound of song they lend;
a blend of hope that all goes down
they beat their drum until the end.

And Santa smiles, he loves to laugh,
his jolly path, his yearly run
will come and go, the day will pass,
his hectic plan has just begun!

(A Seasoned Octet)

Face the Truth

When truth has left a bitter taste
and sours upon the tongue;
we cannot hide from such disgrace,
we must admit we're wrong.

And when we own our memories,
forgiving plays its part;
the only kind of remedies,
are deep within our heart.

So don't deny that truth of it,
as if we do, we'll lose;
to own our deeds, the cap it fits,
no one can be excused.

The trail of blood we leave behind
will dry into the ground;
the stain profoundly leaves a sign
we'll always hear the sound . . .

that beating drum we pounded on,
is ringing in our ears;
the bitter man he had become—
still brings us many tears.

Fake Friends

When someone shows their truest paint,
we take note of their name;
their deed can often scar and taint,
of how they did defame.

No matter what else they may do,
our memory is clear;
once they have crossed the line with you,
your path will always steer.

And others may be fooled by them,
but only you will know;
that they have power to condemn,
this charlatan on show.

Their fake facade is evident,
a smile will never hide
the soul that has been keenly bent—
so they can steal your prize.

Farewell Boris Baby

A fond farewell to Boris baby,
what a ride it's been;
your quirky hair and fairness swayed-me—
you were always keen.

You won with personality--
the den of wolves were hungry;
your individuality
showed you DID serve your country!

You navigated us through hell,
when Covid hit us hard;
as enemies on you would dwell
they criticised and marred.

But I for one think you were great!
You had the toughest job;
at first there was a big debate
but you fought back the mob.

Now that you have a happy grin—
a knighthood's in the wings;
the chaos had us in a spin,
you stood with Knights and Kings.

Feathering your Nest

When feathering one's nest, it is important to remember,
everyone's significant, that's every single member;
communities have cliques, and if you're not part of the club,
develop thicker skin as you are likely to be snubbed.

When gathering your twigs, be very careful which you choose,
the structure of your nest is so important for reviews;
as strong and sturdy branches are the best for good defence,
a delicate interior will make a lot of sense.

But most of all you must keep your integrity intact,
as if you let your anger spill, and squawk with an attack;
you might as well give up the nest as someone will destroy
and scatter remnants all about, and take away your joy.

So always keep an open mind when feathering your nest,
include those newer members who will try to do their best;
and never block someone who has a worthwhile thing to say,
just because you are hell bent on having your own way!

Flamenco

Her every move, emotional,
her body writhes with power
she taps the beat, will not retreat,
until her passions shower;
her skirt is tossed, her temper lost,
her eyes would freeze the soul;
her love is strong, we hear her song,
as she is in control.

The dance advances like a storm,
relentless in pursuit,
with gusto she performs her steps,
the tapping is acute;
the swirling frills, as passion thrills,
and dance becomes an art,
the beating feet is such a treat,
she captures every heart.

Flippin' Pancakes

From frying pans the pancakes flip—
they flop and drop and trip and slip;
they fly like spinning acrobats—
with goo within they spin and splat!

These heavy saucers hit the pan,
and soon they have a golden tan;
they land upon the plate to drown
in maple syrup— berries crown.

Then gobbled up by greedy kids,
expanding waistline, me forbids.
But every now and then I try—
to eat one just before they fly.

Fluttering Murder

Flutter of murder
terror in the sky at night—
empty hearts are cold

Flying the Coop

The Eagle Chick is growing fast,
before he leaves the nest,
behaving independently,
the parents put to test.

They bring him food, fresh from the catch,
ungrateful is his snatch;
a tantrum is displayed to all,
the Mother will detach.

The Chick will fly away too soon,
the hunt and nesting boom,
continues on, as time moves by
in hopeful sunny June.

Observing the behaviour of the Eagles in the nest from a secret camera in California has been fascinating. The young Chick is eager to fly the coop, he practices his flight by spreading his wings pretending to fly. When the parents bring him food he snatches it from them chastising them for taking so long to bring it. The Chick is aggressive, behaving like a teenager in the nest with his frustration. Soon he will be gone and ready to mate with another, as the cycle continues.

Fooled by Love

You left behind some memories,
that keenly sparked with anger;
now time has clouded every spat,
my visions have no anchor.
I can forgive but won't forget,
those moments you refused
to lend a helping hand when I,
was lost and most confused.

You took so selfishly from me,
and drained me of my love—
I felt my strength grow weaker
when I gazed at stars above.
I never felt enriched by love,
as I was fooled by you,
with no togetherness,
as silence fell, and you withdrew.

A legacy of painful thoughts,
left in a trail of loss—
and I was not the only one,
who felt your iron toss.
A frozen spirit, cold to those,
who wanted love much more—
so many broken hearts were left,
in arguments of war.

Now looking back, I learned so much,
about my strength within,
I gained experience that set
me on a course to win.
There are no deep regrets as I
now stand alone with pride,
and never will I let someone,
purloin and leave me tied.

Forever Words

Words etched forever
never to be said or heard
on my Mother's grave

My Mother died aged 82 in 2014, God Rest her Soul.

Friends

We hope to hear the melody
of life's enduring tune,
as long as there's a remedy
for every monsoon;
to never disregard a day,
as each one is a gem,
the rising sun is on display,
we feel the heat again.

We hope to see the blossoming
in spring when trees are bright,
as new life is an awesome thing,
when flowers can excite;
but most of all its friends who tend
and make it all worthwhile—
on those we always can depend,
to bring a happy smile.

Friendlessness

Surrounded by his so-called friends,
he wallows in their praise;
the fake persona never ends,
with actors staging plays.

One day he lost his fortune too,
the word had spread about;
and all those so-called friends he knew,
their time was running out.

Like rats that flee a sinking ship,
these buddies disappeared;
the motivation of these cliques
where patience persevered—

without the pull of rich resources
no one had the time;
as courses made for racing horses,
all were in decline.

You cannot buy a friend my dear
they're born from love and kind;
and men who buy are insincere,
to loneliness confined.

Friendly Musing

When friends become the rock you need,
the ones that never take or feed;
the special people who are there
to share concerns, they're always fair.
The people who are here for keeps
as they bestow their love in heaps;
and if you fall, they pick you up,
and fill your empty, thirsty cup.

Your strength within deserves some praise,
your wicked humour is ablaze,
and I am tickled pink within,
as life's a game we cannot win.
My friend, you have a spirit keen,
alive with wisdom, never mean;
and I for one will welcome you—
with us no subject is taboo.

Frosty Heart

The frost has settled on his heart
with cold uneasiness,
as guilt begins to tear apart
his need for greediness;
the loneliness has sown a seed
of doubtful indiscretion,
although alone his heart will grieve,
there will be no confession.

As he believes he has a right
to walk all over souls,
without a care, puts up a fight,
presides atop controls;
no empathy, the remedy
in silent damning deeds,
ensuring anonymity—
elusively misleads.

The victims wounded, some are dead,
they all remember him;
the heartless torment that he spread,
was oh so very grim;
yet he could never have regrets,
for he was always right,
but mentioning his name upsets—
the horror reignites.

Feuding Neighbours

The fight begins with boundaries,
encroaching over lines;
like careful sewn embroideries,
those errors flag up signs.

An angry shout is put about,
and words feel like they're stones
that pierce the flesh as blood spurts out,
the chill will reach the bones.

Revenge is on the minds of those
who like the tit for tat;
and so a feud is born and grows
into full-blown attack.

Glimpsing Light in Poetry

In words we can reveal ourselves
we tell a tale of woeful spells;
a life, of ups and downs include
the ins and out of what we choose.

The rollercoaster ride of hell
or sweet aroma roses smell
our senses touched in many ways
as words infuse us page by page.

And here I offer up some rhymes,
and tell you of those special times
emotional and factual,
our feelings— international.

A menu— observational
of poems, recreational;
to free the mind of hurtful things
identifying many springs.

So dive inside my words of cheer,
and words of those we hold so dear;
the sorrow and the happiness—
the touch is instantaneous.

Grief Steals Time

I find myself still mourning for you dear,
my loneliness without you sinks my heart;
the challenges of life are full of fear,
as tolerating change tears me apart.

My hope has dwindled with my ageing bones,
no longer can the birds lift with their song,
I drag the burden of my grief like stones
that weigh me down because they are so strong.

But then I hear your voice advising me
to make the most of life, to laugh and sing,
be happy, and enjoy our family—
with all the joys their smiling faces bring.

As life's a gift and we should all be grateful,
to live in deepened sorrow is so wasteful.

(A Sonnet)

Gun Powder Plot

He fought for Spanish armies, was a Catholic, a Traitor.
A planned assassination of King James would be his caper.
In charge of all gunpowder, lay in wait to play his cards;
and blow the King and British Parliament to tiny shards.

A note was sent to Westminster in sixteen zero five,
and Guido was arrested, he was tortured whilst alive.
Confessions were obtained and wicked sentencing decreed,
he would be hung and drawn and quartered, for this dreadful deed.

And Now we have tradition on the fifth day of November.
We burn poor Guy again! And on a bonfire we remember;
The British are barbaric, we set off some fiery works,
to show the world we conquer evil where it lurks it hurts.

The Gunpowder Plot of 1605 was reported to be the most cunning and daring plots in history. It was attempted by forceful Catholics in order to assassinate King James I and destroy parliament in a destructive explosion on the 5th November.

Guy Fawkes, also known as Guido Fawkes was a reformed Catholic born and educated in York and he also fought for the Spanish. He was assigned to guard the explosives beneath the House of Lords. He and another co-conspirator, Robert Catesby planned to set the explosives alight, but an anonymous letter was sent to Westminster alerting them of the plot. Guy Fawkes was arrested, tortured until he confessed and was sentenced to be (hung drawn and quartered), but died from the hanging when his neck was broken.

Since that date England has celebrated (Bonfire Night) on November 5th to commemorate this plot which was avoided and King James I was saved.

Happiness is Priceless

When some are born to misery,
they never see it there,
instead there's opportunity
in everything they share;
the light of day as sun comes up
is what they're grateful for,
to live another day,
anticipating what's in store.

There is no poverty in those
who truly love their life,
they battle every day,
and never think they live in strife.
And no amount of money can
replace the love they feel,
for they will love their children,
in a world that's not ideal.

When some are born to luxury,
they never see it there,
protective of their status,
they will very rarely share;
the focus is on want and greed,
they miss the morning sun,
and shadows form like clouds above,
depression is no fun.

They never yearn for love,
prosperity will be their goal,
the battle is to beat the clock
and gain complete control;
a lavish life will not replace
the loyalty of friends—
in poverty we learn to share,
a trusted hand extends.

Happy 18th Birthday

The moment you took your first breath—
I'm standing at your side;
I've seen you go from strength to strength—
it's been the sweetest ride.

The years have shown, how you have grown—
so tall and bushy tailed;
the years surmount, and life has flown—
a lady now unveiled.

I can't believe that eighteen years—
have flashed before my eyes;
my memories are souvenirs—
that I will always prize.

(For Stella)

Happy Birthday Angela!

Has it really been one year, since posting happy wishes?
Time has move on much too fast, I've washed so many dishes!
Here again we celebrate a birthday just for you—
never will you catch up with my years, or jump the queue!

We have been good closest friends, for many, many days,
know each other's foibles, and each other's funny ways,
every time we speak— we can pick up where we left off—
friends have strong connections, bonds that never ever pop.

Sending you appreciation— for you just being there . . .
sorry I can't share a drink, and show you that I care,
when we meet again we will laugh out loud, and reminisce,
meanwhile on this card there are some hugs, sent with a kiss.

Has Santa Been?

The day arrives, we wake at dawn
don't yawn as it is Christmas morn;
the lawn is frosty, chilled with snow
but in our hearts we want to know.

Has Santa been? His Reindeer keen to fly last night,
as drawn are we to watch the skies, his sleigh so bright.

And children open gifts with glee,
we see the joy in you and me;
the key to happiness begins
when loving hearts hear sleigh bells ring.

(The Tetravalent)

Heads Roll and Queens Rule

Her confidence and clever wit impressed the King of England
vivaciously she courted with a touch of charm that lingered;
and so the King would steer the course of history to suit—
and with the Pope, the King would start a wicked long dispute.

Girls were often pawns in games of power— man's command,
and Anne was keen for status and accepted Henry's hand.
She played the wifely role and Henry took her to his bed,
so happy to submit to him, as now the two were wed.

He won her heart and now this lively lady was his Queen,
she tried to bear a son, instead a girl was on the scene.
Elizabeth was born and learned so much from what she saw,
when heads were lost, such tyranny prevailed in Royal law.

As Henry had a roving eye, was bored with Anne, his wife,
and yearning for another, not so feisty, with less strife.
So Anne, accused of treason, and adultery, was framed,
her fate was sealed, and not appealed, behaviour was acclaimed.

She lost her head, protested that her innocence was real,
but no one listened to her, she submitted to the steel.
What Henry never learned was that his daughter would be Queen—
and ruled the country with a strength that no one else had seen.

Elizabeth, the most courageous Queen in history,
remained a virgin, so that she could rule to victory—
she fought the French, the Spanish and she conquered Scottish sin,
the body of a woman, and stomach of a King.

Henry VIII wanted to divorce his wife Catherine of Aragon to Mary Anne Boleyn. When the Pope refused to grant Henry a divorce, he broke away from the Catholic church and formed The Church of England, a protestant religion. He then married Anne Boleyn.

They had a child, Elizabeth who later became Queen and reigned from (1558-1603) for 45 years. The Greatest Queen who ever lived.

Heartbreaks

A scar exists upon my heart, there is no cure for me,
it happened long ago when my beloved set me free;
I tried to love again, but there are wounds quite deep within,
beneath the skin inside a place where healing can't begin.

Experience has taught me to protect my heart from pain,
to keep the sunshine in and not let storms reach it with rain;
but still the struggle carries on, as hearts are hard to mend,
and only when I love again will all the heartache end.

Then came along a handsome man, and love began to chart,
as love has the capacity to open up the heart;
I felt a certain magic deep inside that made me smile
I knew my heart had healed again, but it took quite a while.

The years went by, my heart was happy with contented beats,
as love gave me some tenderness and lots of lovely treats;
but trouble rumbled at my door that made my heart skip time,
another break I could not take, as mending was a climb.

Alas my heart would break again, the grief shook every limb,
and looking back at life I realised that love within—
is fickle and it's delicate if you expose your hearts,
it's likely that a break will never really mend the marks.

Helmet Hair

I'm not a fan of wearing wigs,
they are so very fake,
but when I saw my hair stylist,
she made a big mistake.
Is that me with a helmet on,
my hair is stiff, won't move,
my flowing locks were stuck right on,
my hair, I disapprove.

My curls look so unnatural,
what happened to my mop?
I look as though I could completely
take my helmet off!
I know I'm getting on in years,
but really? Is this me?
I think I'll wash the lacquer out,
and let my hair be free!

Hidden Beneath the Snow

Thorny roses in my posies—
prick and chew my fingers too;
flow'ring beds don't need those hoses,
heavy snowfall pushes through.

Thought that Autumn was cut shorter,
paid the price, with frozen ice;
as the snow fell on the border,
fluffy cover, white disguise.

Rash from stingers, they are clingers,
as the skin is very thin;
hidden by the snowy slingers;
leaving sore and blotchy sin.

Holly prickling can be crippling,
lethal tykes that I dislike;
hiding under purest stippling,
are those lethal spikes that strike.

(A Hectic Heptad)

Hidden Gems

The musky stench of unwashed clothes that charities now sell,
the cast offs sit inside the shop and incubate the smell;
the trade expands, it's in demand, more clothing than we need,
and money made, can help the brave, so many mouths to feed.

The atmosphere inside the shop is friendly and it's kind,
and many look inside with hope for that great lucky find;
they cross some palms with silver, taking home a hidden gem,
and everybody benefits, recycling scores again.

As Telstar plays an ancient tune to match the age of cloth,
providing meals with clothing deals, no more will they eat broth;
revived are dresses, suits and knits, the clothing sale is endless,
and no one cares who wore these clothes, the profit is tremendous.

Expansion into larger stores these hand me downs are rife—
a garment may have travelled miles to reach the local shelf;
and that is when I spotted— my old Mother's dress— now cold,
a stain was where she left it, and I gave them all my gold.

Hide and Seek

Squirrel tails know how to freeze
and blend into the scenery;
fickle is his expertise
when gaming with his thievery.

Keeping still and statuesque
an art he has perfected here;
leaping, skilful arabesque
he'll wait until the coast is clear.

Camouflaged, no one can spy—
he thinks I cannot spot him there
sabotaged by my keen eye
a photo snapped, means I can share.

(A Rimaric)

Hospital Visit

You take a ticket, then you wait
as numbers buzz upon a screen;
consultants always running late,
impatient men and women scream.

The mood is gloomy, some are rude,
the clock ticks by, and I am bored,
then I am called and I conclude—
my diagnosis has reward.

My body has a few more years
and I continue on my run;
allayed for now are all my fears,
another day to see the sun.

I step into the world outside,
with head held high, no tears to cry;
I dance about just like a child,
so grateful for the azure sky.

Housewives of Beverly Hills

Cat fights, drink nights, dim lights—
hard hearts, worn tarts, fake parts;
loose lips, small hips, short tips,
lost souls, dumb roles, mock robes.

Foul words, plain girls, old birds;
tall pins, crook sins, thick skins,
low life, big hype, bad type—
hoax friends, vogue trends, sad ends.

The Housewives of Beverly Hills is a Netflix production featuring wealthy, long in the tooth (has-been) stars looking for extra fame and to make a bit more money. The show centres on disrespectful bad behaviour from foul mouthed, uneducated women, superficially dressed and disguised as ladies, when in fact they are ugly, uninteresting, scheming, back-biting soulless women who epitomise decadent capitalism at its worst. They drive fancy expensive cars and live in large ostentatious houses and treat their so-called friends like dogs.

Their egos and lack of responsibility taken for their outbursts and gutter language, remind me of a spit and sawdust brawling bar in the backstreets of Glasgow. In fact the guys in those places at least are honest working men.

They think that fake hair extensions, boob implants and plumped up lips disguises their fickle and immoral personalities. This show encourages them to argue and exposes their poor education and low standards, they spit words and throw wine over each other, take drugs and back stab.

They sell their souls to the Devil for money and in return they hide behind expensive clothes and sunglasses to hide their sins. Is this representative of the people who live in LA? This show indulges the whims of women who have no respect for animals. One of them keeps swans in a very small pond for show, dresses dogs in human clothes and allows them to eat and drink at the table! They have a lack of appreciation of others, their surroundings, and they are wasteful, ungrateful and distasteful.

Is this entertainment? I am told this program has a wide audience. I watched to see what it was all about and wrote this poem that accurately describes the show.

How to Score with Words

Write religious poetry
it always hits the spot--
write some words of flattery,
a birthday greet will pop.

Posts that come straight from the heart
of grief and love or sorrow,
will ensure the highest score
to top the charts tomorrow.

Posts about a soldier
or some patriotic stories--
ashes as they smoulder,
fighting for our welcomed glories.

Horror always chills the spine
with tingles left to share;
gory scenes are always fine
with blood and guts in there.

Tell a truthful tale exposing
deeds that are unfair;
as secrets decomposing
are lapped up, when we care.

Clip your words to make them pop,
remember metre reigns,
write your rhymes and never stop
as practice tutors brains.

I Can't Decide

I can't decide?
Is winter here?
Or is it spring?
What time of year?
Or should I shed and go to bed,
or will I flourish here instead.
The earth is cold,
my heart is bold.
Be green,
instead of burnished gold.
What should I do,
the trees are bare
and all I want to do is share.

So I decided,
I would be, the only tree
to look like me!

A two tone colour,
here to stay,
I'll teach the other trees today.
Be gay,
not gold,
let green take hold,
despite the winter
and the cold.

Add colour
to your repertoire,
the green against
the snow will star!

Alas, my leaves
are falling down,
and I no longer
wear the crown.

Ignorance

We blame if all on ignorance
the lack of true respect;
as tossed are words, belligerent
a view that they project.

So short on understanding here
they know not what they do;
the wrangling can be so severe,
and very hard to chew.

If only people did a search
and learned about events;
perhaps they would not try and lurch
into such arguments.

I'm just Like my Dad

I want to be just like my Dad,
he wears a soldiers suit;
his hunting skills I have to add,
are never in dispute.

For he is king of all the sky,
I see him fly above;
so proud am I, and this is why
my Dad I really love.

One day I shall look just the same,
my head will be bright white;
my beak of sunshine yellow fame
a really well dressed Knight.

And I'll return to nest in trees
to nurture chicks like you;
a legacy with guarantees—
my debut will come true.

In the Light of the Moon

In the light of a moon that is full,
I can whisper to trees in the night;
and my shadow will frighten the wolf
as I am so much taller in height.

And the stars have a habit of falling,
in love with the moon as they ride;
and this magical eve there's a stirring,
an Owl has his eye on his bride.

I can hear gentle hooting and smooching
the wolf is as still as a rock;
and my shadow soon fades as the mooning
now covered by cloud so's to block.

I'm no longer a threat to the evening,
and the wolf is no longer so scared;
as the couple in trees are believing—
their vows mean they'll always be paired.

Indifference

Indifference cuts deep like silent blades,
invisible our presence when it strikes;
it's cold and calculated, it invades—
and spreads its tentacles in tiny bites.

We are not heard our voice falls on deaf ears,
and ignorance joins forces in the plight;
we might as well be dead, there are no tears
no point retaliating, there's no fight.

Detached impassive waves of insolence,
has power in its quiet vacant stare—
and no one else will notice indolence,
it creeps into the bones and will impair.

To break the apathy and show concern—
we have to teach indifference to learn.

(A Sonnet)

Injustice Lives

When accidents occur we always want someone to blame,
a scape goat, any fool will do, to let our temper aim;
a target for our grief, an outlet for our inner hurt,
and some will hang because we let our anger hurl the dirt.

The media, the law, condemns— a man is put to death—
We're quick to make decisions, take another person's breath;
when truth becomes apparent, no one wants to make amends—
as based upon assumption, unresolved are open ends.

And jumping to conclusions never solves a crime my dear,
the puzzle needs the pieces, like a jigsaw, to be clear;
no guessing this or that, as only fact will serve the truth,
so never point the finger without having all the proof.

The facts, the evidence is what we need to win the race,
and not some silly housewife with a hunch she solved the case;
as every man deserves the fairness of unbiased trials,
when measuring injustices, the files will stretch for miles.

Inspiration is Everywhere

When staring at the blankness of a page
and finding inspiration with no clues;
a beam of sunlight magically staged,
ignites imagination with its hues.

Before too long a poem has been formed,
no longer is the page untouched by words;
the smallest change in mood can be transformed,
we are enlightened by things most absurd.

Relax and let the life around you soar,
and in a moment, you will find the source
to write a wistful poem with a core—
that resonates with others with its cause.

As time moves forward change is evident,
the smallest detail can be relevant.

(A Sonnet)

Invasion

As lies pour in about this sin,
and leaders have their say;
this action speaks a thousand words—
dishonour's on display.

Invasion cannot be denied
although the lies were told;
the truth reveals the tale is bold,
as history unfolds.

We have a tyrant in our midst,
a madman at the helm;
his story had so many twists—
deceit can overwhelm.

When one man stays in charge too long
he loses grip on life;
a selfishness that sings a song
of terror and of strife.

The tension of destructive fear
has filled some hearts with sorrow
with bombs and troops that bring a tear
to eyes with no tomorrow.

And life will never be the same,
for those who have been caged;
a jumped-up coward is to blame,
the world around enraged.

It's a Dog's Life

I've been around the block and always know my way around,
don't need to be a greyhound with my nose against the ground;
instinctively I know a crisis, guess the outcome too—
when you're as wise as me, then you will know just what to do.

I take a walk around the garden, let the crisis pass—
and lift my leg to mark my territory upon the grass.
When voices have subsided and they all sit down to eat,
I look at them with puppy eyes until they give a treat.

Dynamics in this family— I sit right in the middle,
democracy means no one tries to threaten or belittle.
So in my own back yard I am the King of all I see,
and confidence is something that you'll always see in me.

A creature of routine, I love my daily country walks,
and trouble follows me when I am on that muddy course,
as what's the point in going out, if you can't splash about,
with puddles everywhere it's fun to wet my face and snout.

Exhausted now and hungry, I return to eat my feed,
and in my comfy bed I have just everything I need;
I sleep until I hear the rattle of my doggy chain,
as I can go and play again in pouring English rain.

It's Beginning to Feel a Lot like Christmas

(A Parody)

It's beginning to feel a lot like Christmas
not that we have snow—
Take a look in the shops 'til 10, purchasing once again
with fairy lights and baubles all on show.

It's beginning to feel a lot like Christmas,
boys think it's a chore,

but the silliest sight to see, and I'm sure you will agree
no cards through your front door!

The postal disputes mean I won't get my boots,
and my card won't reach number ten,
polls are just talk and can go for a walk
the Crown is in trouble within—
As Megan has the gall to do an interview again!

It's beginning to feel a lot like Christmas
not that we have snow—
There's a fee when you kiss and tell, making an awful smell,
the sturdy kind that doesn't mind the show.

It's beginning to feel a lot like Christmas
soon the hell will start
and the thing that'll make it sting is the mud that she will sling
right within her heart.

It's beginning to feel a lot like Christmas,
strikes are such a chore
but the silliest sight to see, and I'm sure you will agree
no cards through your front door!

Sure, it's Christmas once more!

In 2022, with have postal strikes in England causing chaos at Christmas and Megan and Harry are about to air on Netflix with another betrayal for the Palace to defend.

Jet Setting

To fly up high above the cloud,
enveloped shroud of fluffy white;
the sight of silver cresting proud,
a glimpse of sky that's glittered bright.

A bird of metal packed with folk
exchange the soak for sunny climes;
to try, recharge a bit of hope—
select a word, describe with rhymes.

Across the globe we venture out,
and jet about the big wide world;
I heard an eagle has some doubt,
as flying's not just for a bird.

(A Seasoned Octet)

Just a Little Girl in Trouble

She was never a wild child,
a quiet girl with few words to say,
a vulnerable and delicate soul
at the mercy of men's lustful eyes.

Friends asked her to dress up a bit and hit the town,
she agreed, what harm could it do?

Two strong drinks went straight to her head,
a fine young gentleman helped guide her way
to the ladies room—
her light-head and unsure steps
made her fall into his arms.

He had very different ideas
and she soon found herself
outside up against a brick wall in an alleyway.
"Please" she said, "let me go back to my friends".
He whispered: "of course, in just a moment".

A moment was all it took to penetrate this virgin child,
as she was powerless to fight back.

The following weeks proved difficult
as she admitted to her parents—
she was pregnant.

Now she was just a little girl in trouble.
Alone and desperate.

Keep a Watchful Eye

Accept the fact that strife is constant when you are alive,
because of this, discord will come, we all want to survive.
Unless you live inside a tent, on land that feeds your soul,
you'll pay the bills, and fight the tills when they ring up the toll.

You may ride on a treadmill, multiplying is the speed,
and getting off is not a choice, as earning pays for greed.
An active phone, computer, tantalising as they taunt,
to show you what you're missing and the trap is set, you're caught.

The fakers try to dip into your purse with mock emails,
and you may lose your house, your car— ignoring these details!
As life on earth is complex if you're living in the city,
and even on a farm, your bank account may not look pretty.

There is no real escape from life, when earth is run on funds,
and everyone is stealing from you— they're not using guns!
You have to stay so vigilant and keep a watchful eye,
as even someone innocent could be a thief or spy.

Keeping up Appearances

My Mother taught me lessons here, in how to look my best,
to never let a grief-filled day be pressurised by your stress;
appearances were everything, the face we hide behind,
expressing sorrow, crying out, means we are not refined.

But then I found my poetry! I write down how I feel,
my smile is showing happiness, but words here will reveal;
the lie exposed in rhyming words, the fake facade is cracked,
as private tears now wet the page, my metaphors react.

The truth is that we're all the same, our hearts can often break,
and sharing inner thoughts with friends is never a mistake;
we cannot hide behind a smile when it's not genuine,
we only heal when we reveal what's hurting deep within.

So read my words and know that I uncover all my flaws,
my vulnerable heart and soul has flimsy paper walls;
I want the world to see my passion, learn that I am strong,
although I might enjoy my fashion, words reveal my song.

Kids Love the Snow

With no apology, the snow
with tiny flakes of lacy ice
fell high and low across the land
and soon enticed the kids to throw.

They ran about and soon began
to slip and slide a downward ride,
without a plan the children said:
"we love to glide fast as we can!"

The falling flakes don't please us all,
as bitter frost can bite our toes;
but little balls of snow are fun,
no winter woes when we are small.

(The Cryptic Labyrinth)

Kill that Word!

When I was young I read a book that told us of a word
that never should be used as it was lazy and absurd;
since then the word kept creeping into sentences and phrases,
I couldn't shake this dirty weed that terminated praises.

This word that rhymes with blot would haunt me every time I spoke,
its tentacles had strangled me and almost made me choke.
Why does a word exist when it cannot be used at will?
But lessons learned when I was young persistently, they chill.

As often when this word is used, it makes itself redundant,
as taking out this word, a better sentence is resultant;
experiments performed would prove this word should not be used,
yet often those who use this word are pardoned and excused.

But I remain still faithful to the teaching long ago,
and pluck this word out like a weed to let my roses grow;
to let my poems thrive, allow my prose to never rot,
the irksome and offensive word that steals your soul is GOT!

Kindred Spirits, my Cat and Me

Adventurous and lithe was he—
his eyes were wide, he watched with glee;
he never missed a single trick,
I knew what made his ego tick.
His liberty was everything
and in the street he was a King.
He ruled the town, he wore the crown—
his reputation was renown.

His instinct, wild, unruly too,
so self-sufficient, through and through,
our independence here was shared—
he was like me, and never scared.
We kindred spirits loved our life,

and battled with a sim'lar strife,

as both of us would play the game-
our eyes were on the prize to claim.

As each of us could pull a stunt.
when both of us were on the hunt.
with me for bargains, him for mice,
although the mice would pay the price.
And like me, he would cuddle close,
and purred for longing, loving strokes.
When days were done, he could retire—
beside the embers near the fire.

Know What you are Talking About

A lesson Father taught me, and I hear his words speak out,
before critiquing someone else, learn first— before you spout;
and research, be prepared for questions, never speaking first,
or go head long into a meeting when you're unrehearsed.

To know your subject, always be ahead of what's to come,
just like a game of chess, look straight ahead, or you'll succumb;
not everybody has a sense of fairness in their stride,
and some will cheat and lie and all your rights will be denied.

So if your feet become too big to wear your well-worn boots,
then you must do your homework, to resolve those big disputes;
and speak when you have confidence and know your subject well,
as if a word is out of turn, you will go straight to hell.

Landing with a Bump

The destination far away—
a flight will need to climb;
when jet propelled into the sky
the slow ascent takes time.

Just like a bird on moonlit nights
we landed in the dark;
a bump upon the tarmac bites
and friction gave a spark.

The jolting forward was a pain
and knocked us all about;
the pilot did not like the rain,
he could not see much out.

But we survived and reached our goal
we landed in one piece;
the silver bird held many souls,
whose heartbeats had increased!

Learning from History

When born to liberty and wealth
we're blind to others' needs;
with benefits of youthful health,
unseen is death— disease.

And only when we're touched in life,
by poverty and chains,
can we begin to fathom strife
and understand its pains.

Our blinkers stop us seeing truth,
too focused on our own;
my wish is that we teach our youth
the history we've known.

The ups and downs, the big mistakes,
the sorrows and the pain;
the wars, the cause, the sharks and snakes,
torrential is the rain.

We can't escape our dreadful deeds,
our dumb insanity;
attending to our human needs,
to save humanity.

Leaving . . .

There were no words, her lips were closed
she left him in her bed;
determined she was so composed,
she walked away from dread.

There was no love left in her heart,
as ice had formed instead;
and leaving was the hardest part,
complete change was ahead.

The fear of loneliness was keen
her strength was weakening;
but memories of what had been
were really sickening.

With every step her courage dared--
and soon she felt the breeze
caressing every lock of hair
no longer ill at ease.

Lend an Ear

Defined by our experience
not all of it is good—
and marked are we, there's no pretence
not always understood.

Some cope with trauma, find the time
to see the truth within,
and pigeon hole emotion, climb—
develop thicker skin.

But most of us are hit too hard
by death and grief and pain;
and putting on a fake facade
won't hide the stormy rain.

If we can share anxiety
and lend a friend our ear;
develop our society—
distress might disappear.

Let Those Voices Sing

When nothing lasts forever here
and time destroys the past;
we forage forward with a cheer
to beat the stone that's cast.

Why do we have good memory,
to haunt along the way;
when time's designed so cleverly
to steal our yesterday?

To focus on our forward step
means never looking back;
the tragedy and grief we've met,
can constantly attack.

When locked inside the maze of life
we lose our precious breath,
the past events cut like a knife,
before too long there's death.

So free yourself from shackled chains,
add pearls to every string;
and try to stay inside the lanes,
to let those voices sing.

The time is now, our sense renewed,
we see, we hear so much;
our heart is open to include--
those present times we touch.

Let Your Talent Shine

Let talent shine right through your words
we listen to your nouns and verbs;
your sentiment will touch our heart
and bring a tear and tear apart.

So pen a word and sing your song,
reviews will surely come along;
we need to hear your point of view,
so write more than a word or two.

No matter what you have to say
please put your poems on display;
and I will seek and look and find
the best will not be left behind.

And if your purse has no more coppers—
I will find all your show stoppers;
sixes are reserved for you!
So write and make your first debut!

To all those newbies, grab a pen
use that paper, write again;
I want to read you for two cents,
as talent here can be immense.

(A Tribute to "Fanstory", an on-line Poetry Site encouraging new authors to write and create, receive critique and advice from the more experienced members)

Lichfield Cathedral

For centuries those faithful spires,
have overlooked the town;
the chiming bells and tuneful choirs,
have spread the word around.
On sacred ground where faith again,
has comforted the people,
from far and wide, in mist and rain,
we view each forthright steeple.

The heart of Lichfield beats in her,
she magically beams,
reflecting shadows, I concur,
with purpose she redeems.
She quells the fear when we feel odd,
with some dysphoria;
When entering the house of God,
we feel euphoria.

Lies Spread like Flies

The gossips love to tell a tale,
the whispering that makes us wail;
the poison planted with its venom—
adding to the chat addendum.

The seed that packs a mighty punch,
disturbing everybody's lunch,
and as the rot begins to grow,
encouraging the word to blow . . .

an eye of newt and toe of frog,
the wool of bat and tongue of dog,
a cauldron stirs with double trouble,
gossips love to burst our bubble.

When rumours fly around like bats,
there is no need for witches hats;
inside the mind of those who talk,
is someone who enjoys to stalk.

The tittle-tattle spread with tongue,
will stick to you like cow pat dung;
the smell will never go away—
and stain your heart with its decay.

And if you stir your wooden spoon,
and join the witches in their swoon,
you'll have a target on your back—
no one will trust you, that's a fact.

Life

When life brings days of anxious thoughts
that build inside our mind,
our hearts can break when we are caught
in love, we can be blind.

We walk along our chosen path
believing it is good,
and when we feel the hand of wrath,
we curse the seeded bud.

Exposed are ears to sounds and fears
and eyes will witness sorrow,
and with emotion shed some tears,
as grief can thwart tomorrow.

With hope and faith our future mends,
we bear the scars with pride;
and learn to navigate the bends,
and try to steer the ride.

Life and Death

How could I forget you dearest
though it's been so long ago;
visions blurry, not the clearest,
I still miss your to and fro.

Commentary: cricket blaring—
racing horses, football roars;
tinkling glasses, wine we're sharing—
kissing, hugging, so restores.

Suns are setting on our lifespan,
days in Summer are long gone;
Winter claims, I'm not a big fan—
but I know I will succumb . . .

following inside your footsteps
Heaven's gate is open now—
I will join you one day, don't stress
fate and destiny is how.

Life and Times

Time has a habit of churning,
and moving too fast when we're old;
images of us all learning
now turning to treasures in gold.

This is the cycle of living,
we keep alive every detail;
history never forgiving
with days on our winding long trail.

Breathe in the air, smell the fragrance
as time steals each minute out there;
capture a memoire, have patience,
and never miss moments to share.

Life Outdoors

I lean against the old oak tree
the sun is low, there is no shade,
the light will fade, I will not see
as darkness reigns on my parade.

I will not move when it gets dark,
this spot is where I'll sleep tonight;
and rising with the early lark,
the sun will warm me when it's light.

Do not think me a homeless man,
I choose to live outside with bees
and birds who entertain and can
uplift my mood, they always please.

I lean against the old oak tree
in winter when the snow is cold;
although I'm always free to see—
with nature I am growing old.

So if you see me in the park,
Don't frown as I am not like you—
I'm not afraid of cold and dark,
I'm here to just enjoy the view.

Life's Tangled Web

Inside a spiders web there is a fly that can't escape,
and caught within a trap his fate is sealed, make no mistake;
the struggle may continue, but the fly will not be free,
as nature will dictate its fate, there is no guarantee.

We never know our destiny, tomorrow holds the key,
for what life has in store for us, remains a mystery;
avoiding all the pitfalls to ensure we still stay safe,
and not become entangled in a web to seal our fate.

Lifestyle Changes

When young, we are so eager to grow up and conquer all,
our strides are long and forceful and we answer every call;
in time we learn that exercise is taken every day,
to keep us moving as we age to keep the aches at bay.

When ageing causes tiredness, as lethargy's a curse,
we may lack sleep, a zombie be, or maybe something worse;
as energy is drained from every muscle, every bone--
we fail to sleep in peace when aches and pains bring on a moan.

One day I will be overcome with tiredness and sit,
and when this day arrives I will succumb and will admit
that taking exercise will be confined to only walking,
as long as I can meet my friends and still do all the talking!

Lineage

A predator in female form,
her stare could curdle cream;
her anger has the fire of Rome,
she has great self-esteem.

Her tattooed arms and pig-ringed nose—
her pumped up lips and breasts;
bleached spiky hair and purple clothes,
a tongue that never rests.

She's screaming at the little kids,
and chokes on cigarettes;
this rag tag Mother's full of fibs—
her duty she forgets.

Behaviour like you've never seen,
four letter words are spat;
her five year old has ears quite keen,
and shares this tit for tat.

She laughs out loud and praises him,
he'll grow up in her image;
a rag tag boy with hate within,
aggression makes me grimace.

The two of them will draw in smoke,
the younger turns to drugs;
the breeding process goes for broke,
and thick are these two bloods.

Little Things in Life

It's the little things in life,
that matter most—
that smile that you remember
and that letter through the post.
The flower pressed with love
and the words that someone wrote.

When another heart can touch
from far away—
a message that's so tender,
now their card is on display.
The warmth that someone feels—
sending happiness my way.

When surprises bring us joy
they are serene—
I'm conveying to the sender
my good wishes that are keen
to read and be so moved
by the love that's in between.

Living High in New York

Commissions are the biggest gain
and life's insane when buying space;
the pace is fast, you have to train,
the war is brisk, no time to waste.

The listing has but weeks to sell,
it can be hell to find a guy;
who wants to buy a place to dwell,
when homes insists on being high.

And living in the sky will cost,
inside a loft apartment here;
it's clear that money has been tossed
an unforgiving pioneer!

Manhattan scrappers touch the stars,
New York's bazaar has painted clouds;
the ground has gone, no sound of cars,
in high rise flats, above the crowds.

With neighbours who are millionaires,
the space they share in concrete skies;
defies all gravity upstairs—
it's not okay to compromise.

The only way to live is up
no interruptions in the air;
and staring out I am quite struck—
the skylines shown, are always shared.

(A Seasoned Octet)

Living Well

Fickle is the light of life as it can dim with age,
listen to your inner voice, not let it fill with rage;
life is worthy of good praise and some will die too young,
secrets of a longer life are held inside a song.

Attitude and gratitude will stand you in good stead,
life is full of woeful song, so try to keep your head.
Concentrate your mind and meditate to calm your soul,
eat a healthy diet, and maintain some self-control.

Always exercise and climb the stair, don't take the lift,
every step you take will keep your body strong and fit.
Lastly keep your smile on show whenever you go out,
happiness requires a heart that's powerful and stout.

Long Lost Daughter

In every smile he saw a trait,
relating to the big debate;
was fate about to change this girl
was she her Daddy's special pearl?

The daughter he'd been looking for,
a door had opened to explore;
before a word was spoken here,
his heart was skipping with a cheer.

He watched in silence as his future changed for good,
a state of pure excitement, now he understood.

The girl who left him long ago—
a glow of life inside so slow—
had grown up to be beautiful,
if only he'd been dutiful.

(The Tetravalent)

Loss and Grief

Loss and grief are buried deep
inside a heart that breaks in two—
crossing over into sleep
will leave behind the strongest glue.

Eulogies hang in the breeze
and sing a song from long ago;
jubilees are memories
as tears begin to overflow.

Crushing sorrow can control
and kind support will help us see—
touching words will soothe our soul
and in our prayers, let go, be free.

(A Rimaric)

Loss Lives On

If only life had granted us
a few more precious hours;
to dance the samba, make a fuss
before death deftly sours.

A moment longer to recoup
the love that lingered here;
in order to regain, regroup
a memory of cheer.

Alas, I'll never see your face
or hear your words again;
or feel your tender warm embrace,
or taste your lips— dear Ken.

But I remember many days
when you were by my side;
your quirky, pleasant, funny ways
.inside me still reside.

Love and Loss

When love can soothe the mind and soul, the body feels the joy,
we trust our instinct, play the role, our hearts are never coy,
the trust will build a bond within, that lasts a lifetime too,
and nothing shakes the union, that two lovers know is true;

and over time this tie so strong will conquer strife and pain,
togetherness means that we belong, we weather snow and rain;
forever love will be remembered, etched upon our heart,
we felt the grief in late December, when we were apart.

The seasons mark the time and place, our senses never fail,
uniquely we all feel the same, as death can end the tale.
The silence rules our head and heart, no noise can filter through,
alone the love no longer charts, the emptiness— acute.

Love Began to Die

The Autumn love of rustic browns,
the mood of discontented frowns;
as changes took another path
that silenced every single laugh.

I never could identify,
or find a reason, when or why,
but when the shroud grew thick and fast
I knew our love would never last.

And when the winter snow set in,
I felt the chill upon my skin,
but most of all my broken-heart
meant we would always be apart.

Love is all Around

I once felt love, a daily gift,
that never stopped its giving,
I took for granted every lift,
that helped me with my living—
but then one day the love was gone,
and left alone was I,
I never had the chance to even say my last goodbye.

Now looking back at times when love
would greet me every day,
the warmth of it, I must admit,
a magical bouquet—
that fed me with the kind of fuel
to face the world outside,
I cannot seem to live now that I know that love has died.

But then I look and see the doves
are mating, love is rife—
and in the spring when flowers bloom,
they take away my strife;
and love is all around me, I
just need to see and share—
as love can come in many forms, there's so much love out there.

Love needs Praise

I never thought my love was wasted here—
I gave my all and don't regret a thing;
the disappointment comes from lack of cheer,
as love was not enough to make you sing.

You wanted so much more, to own my soul,
my spirit, it was crashed beneath the rubble;
and damned was I to life lived on my own,
as loving you would only bring me trouble.

Now ash lies in the hearth where flames were bright,
I do not have regret, as life was true;
although I miss the company at night,
I know that I can never be with you.

As I would praise our love, you saw divide,
the lack of loyalty would end the ride.

(A Sonnet)

Love's Short Promise

The love that we have started now has wings,
the atmosphere is warm and I feel free,
my step is light, within my heart it sings;
increasing passion deep inside of me.

The promises we've made, cement our bond,
and months turn into years together now;
it's us against the world, as we are strong,
and marriage has become our sacred vow.

But you were called by God, he needed you—
we never said goodbye, there was no time;
my empty bed is cold, as all I knew
was stolen from me with no warning sign.

As I reflect on my life's stormy weather
what little happy time we had together.

(A Sonnet)

Lovely Lia

In harmony she glides upon the bluest Grecian sea,
her bow is parting waves, her sails catch winds completely free;
this Jaguar negotiates the swells and mighty storms,
and bobs about the ocean bed when frothy waving forms.

I sailed around the harbour and enjoyed a sunny day,
and moored with mighty ships was dwarfed by them inside the bay.
I'll not forget the moments that would gnaw into my mind,
how sad I was to see another fad be left behind.

The skipper sold her as it was too hard to sail this boat,
as it required some dedication, she had lost his vote;
and I expect she sails again in waters deep and blue,
a crew on board who know that she is capable and true.

Lucinda + Nanny McPhee

Oh Nanna you're always so happy,
and even when life's looking shabby;
your smile brings a flair
as you're always there,
still bringing some charm to the alley.

With your sunny smile, I am cheery,
with your fun loving attitude dearie;
the skip in your step,
makes me quite adept,
whenever I meet you— see clearly . . .

together we smash every problem,
not gloomy or sad, never solemn;
we dance every day
we both have our say
and jointly we are rather awesome!

(A Trio Limericks)

Lucy Lou is Ten

Now you are ten, I took my pen,
to write a tale or two,
about a girl who loves to twirl,
and dance and sing— it's true!
She likes to climb, and all the time,
she whispers to the trees—
I'll hang onto your branches,
and I won't disturb your leaves!

She lands on hands with her handstands,
and legs a cartwheel pose,
and kicks a ball, as I recall,
her footballing bestows—
a skilful, wilful dedication,
to the art of soccer . . .
scoring goals with her controls,
and nothing here will stop her!

An artist, writer, poetess,
she pens a loving word—
in every note she gets my vote,
my eyesight's often blurred—
she darts about, the years surmount,
and I just can't keep up!
But this I know, I love the show—
another leap and jump!

Magical Metre

If your poem's out of kilter
try to get it back on track;
it could mean you've lost the metre,
putting rhythm out of whack.

Try to hear the song within it,
telling you there's something wrong;
fixing metre is the secret—
making every message strong.

Anchor all you thoughts with rhyming,
tap the beat to hear the sound;
poetry relies on timing,
put your words the right way round.

Those who add that extra icing
make a cake that tastes real good;
recipes can be surprising,
when your metre's understood.

Malone, the Scary Cat

The cat sees all on Halloween
he's keen to spook the rat;
but when the bat screams his routine
he's preened for the attack.

His name's Malone he rules the street
he won't allow a trick or treat.

The graves are full of ghostly bones
the moans of deadly braves;
these are the slaves beneath the stones,
Malone then misbehaves.

(A Pinned Decimal)

Meet and Greet

Meet at the quay?
I plod along the mile long beach—
meet at the quay.
The sunset shimmers, out of reach
where azure skies will greet the sea.
Will you be there? No guarantee—
meet at the quay.

(A French Rondelet)

Memories of Grief

When you had somewhere else to go,
my sun was dulled by cloud you know;
the shock of death steals all the fun
and all I wanted was to run.

But no one can escape the grief,
just like a shock, it is a thief;
and looking back, the silence stilled
I shook with terror, fear had chilled.

The blow of it still haunts my mind
as you were always good and kind;
as I remember all you did,
those memories of how we lived.

I've learned to live without your love
and know you watch me from above;
my darkest days are in the past,
I live with hope that grief will pass.

Because the sun eclipsed that day,
I've tried to recreate a way
of introducing joy and fun
and from the pain, no longer run.

I've faced my fears and dried my tears,
and I've enjoyed my recent years;
and when I think of what we had
my memories are never sad.

Memories of my Father

The flapping final curtain falls and stills the chilling night,
he died as he had lived with hope and optimistic fight;
but when the reaper stamps your card, it's time to say goodbye,
you left us all and scarred our hearts with sorrow in your cry.

Remembering your forward stride to keep on moving on
you never let the grass grow underfoot, you saw the sun;
bombarded your way through so that you won and made your mark,
and up before the rest, your personality had spark.

If only you had noticed me, encouraged me in life,
I seemed to be invisible, you only saw the strife;
now you are gone I'm looking back at times we should have shared,
but ego played a part in you that left me unprepared.

I blamed you for shortcomings, now I own my faults and know,
that life is what you make it and we all must join the show;
embrace each day and make the most of all life has to give,
and most of all we learn the truth is that we must forgive.

Inherent are the traits you left inside my heart and soul,
but tempered with compassion, I have let go of control;
allow my friends and neighbours, my family have their say
without a judging word I try to steer them on their way.

I miss you as your large as life determination won,
and no one lives forever, and by death you were outrun;
I gaze above and see the shooting stars up in the sky
you're looking down at me with your advice in good supply.

Mending Hearts

I sense a wrong in everything I try and do,
yet I know nothing of my crime or wrongful deed;
if only you could speak to me and my mind feed,
I would then change my actions, listening to you.

I realise that you are in distress here too,
and body language told me, I must heed the seed;
but I cannot correct or know how to proceed,
my heart is breaking seeing you so sad and blue.
So tell me now what can I do? To make you change?
As love is lost just now, and we are both estranged.

A talk would help to heal the rift that's grown within,
and we can mend our friendship, tend our treasuries;
return to what we had and build more memories,
and bond with magic once again, as we are kin.

(A French Sonnet)

Metalwork

Those who made the metal bend into an artful pose,
soon inject some life into a stone cold pipe or hose;
heated, treated sheets become as soft as plasticine,
pliable, reliable, a metal figurine!

Cogs then melt into a welt, are scarred so permanently,
statuesque and arabesque, in waves so turbulently;
scattered patterns, battered, flattened into shapes we know,
artist's eyes will compromise, solid metals flow.

Sheets of dead and dormant foil revived by skilful hands,
shadows of the past reformed from empty latent cans;
presented with finesse are objects pulled and pushed by heat,
sworn to be transformed into an ornament now neat.

Never cold or old or sold for tuppence ha'penny,
priceless pieces held in high esteem by oh so many;
objects of desire are made from raw and ugly metal,
articles now delicate— made from an unloved kettle.

Miracles in Life

Tinsel glints on sunny days, it's dull when light defers;
magic happens when a little miracle occurs;
butterflies cocooned inside a hanging chrysalis,
never realising, this is quite miraculous.

Eggshells broken by a chick that know just when to hatch,
seeds produce a sapling, over time there is a branch;
flowers know to follow sunny beams until they die
earth goes round the sun and night and day just pass us by.

Bees produce the honey, and the cow provides the milk,
cotton grows abundantly, we make good use of silk;
everywhere we look there is a miracle performed,
over centuries our world has changed, it has transformed.

Life is positive and never ever gives up hope,
miracles are magnified within our telescope;
taking life for granted, as there is no guarantee,
watch and learn as life is fine, there is so much to see.

Moles

Moles love holes, make mounds, no sounds—
dig down, don't drown, wear frumpy frowns.

Tick and tock, they never ever stop,
and air is shared beneath the plot.

Turn the soil, they toil and spoil,
and farmers never seem to foil

Overnight these knights at work
they cultivate and poke the dirt.

Digging deep they keep their cool,
allowing water through, not pool.

Moles love holes, make mounds, no sounds,
dig down, don't drown, wear frumpy frowns.

Moles dig up the earth and help make the soil healthier by aerating it. Allowing plants to grown to feed more insects. Their tunnels also help improve soil drainage which stops flooding and huge puddles forming on the ground.

Mona is Moaning

That smile is worth its weight in gold
if grins can weigh on scales;
but some graffiti casts great doubt
on all those fine details.

As modern scrawl appals us all
as youthful wings spread doubt,
and daub the walls, a painted sprawl,
to shout opinion out.

And here the two contrasting tastes,
in conflict with each other,
we ponder over such debates,
the wash of vibrant colour.

Tradition fights against the splash
of pop artistic vibe;
a clash of culture might be trash—
or is it art transcribed?

Monster Roller Coaster

The monster structure, tall and wide, stood firm like rods of steel,
it rattled like a poisoned snake, with rails to hold each wheel;
against the sky it ruled the earth and beckoned every child—
to take a ride up to the Gods and plummet, screaming, wild.

We climbed the steps up to the car and sat on stone cold seats,
a bar was placed upon our laps, we gave up our receipts;
the ratchet ticked and pulled the can up to the highest point,
the tiny people down below then waved as they rejoiced.

As silence fell we saw the hell, the steep declining horror.

I wondered why I'd paid a fee to test this Terror Momma,

The iron creaked, my daughter shrieked, the fear was evident,
the ride of metal set to scare— it was malevolent.

The car released, the speed increased, I shuddered with the blow,
the mayhem hit, my heart it skipped, and downward we did go.
my flapping skin with wrinkles in had just received a surge,
the wind struck hard, my knees were jarred, we teetered on the verge.

And when the ride was over, I regained my faith in God,
as I survived this manic ride and so did all my squad.
"Again, again", my daughter said, I turned a paler shade,
don't push your luck, this metal truck has had its last crusade.

Mothers

We're scarred and flawed by bruises in our life,
and take responsibility to heart;
when faced with hardships, we give into strife
not every family has chance to chart.

As Mothers hold the reins and steer their children,
so unprepared are they for duties here—
and every now and then, one in a million
successfully will guarantee a cheer.

But Motherhood is not for everyone—
and learning on the job can be so hard,
especially when they don't see the sun,
experience has put them on their guard.

Mistakes are made, emotions can be high
we never get to choose who Mothers us;
and looking at events that made us cry—
forgiving and forgetting halts the fuss.

Remembering we did our very best,
we only get one Mother, don't forget;
and every Mother will endure the test,
to win or fail, there must be no regret . . .

for every child will push those boundaries,
a cycle that's been here for centuries.

Mourning Yesterday

Oh how I mourn for yesterday,
those golden days when you were small,
and in the garden we would play,
now you have grown so very tall.

I'd give my arm to turn the clock
to hug my child just one more time;
the years have flown and ran amok,
I'm looking back when you were mine.

Alas the ticking clock moves on,
enjoy those previous times I say,
as time will steal, and it will con
and soon you'll dream of yesterday.

Mozzies

They work in pairs or even threes
or maybe fours when on a siege;
they organise their panther troops
they charge like mighty nincompoops.

You hear the buzzing in your ears
and soon there will be painful tears;
their landing craft is delicate—
you'll never even feel the cut.

Then suddenly you sense the pain
as blood reveals a tiny stain—
these vampires can anaesthetise
and lumpy skin is on the rise.

They float about like ruthless thugs—
a flying threat, these brutal bugs,
and swatting them is such a chore
you hit one and there is one more!

Disease is spread as they inject
they rage inside their vile neglect;
and suck your blood and plant a seed,
you won't forget that fearful bleed.

Be well prepared before the raid,
use potent DEET to stop their trade!
so wear it when it's hot and sticky
Mozzies can be very tricky!

My Garden Walk

The York— Lancaster Roses sent a thousand to their death,
yet innocent are Roses when we think of Juliet;
The Cuckoo-buds of yellow paint, the meadow with delight,
and Daisies dot the grass with petals of the purest white.

Accompanied by Poppies floating on the tender breeze,
and Rosemary fills noses with a memory that frees.
As Lavender and Mints invite us all to savour time,
and Marjoram is wild and questions why is it a crime.

And I enjoy the Hemlock as it has a darker side—
the Dandelion seeds that travel through the air, sublime;
the Clover and the Blackberry, the Holly, Ivy too—
the flowers, they are everywhere, bring joy to me and you.

My Legacy

If I can leave a legacy within my every word,
I will include the things I've loved inside this wondrous world;
the people who have helped me see that I am capable,
support I have received from them has been so wonderful.

So many thank you's I would give, especially to those—
who love my mind, admire my rhymes and words that I propose;
the teachers and my friends who have stood by me all the way,
I owe them everything as they are still my friends today!

The things I now rely on are my glasses and my phone,
I wouldn't be without my watch, and keys to my new home;
I keep a little book of verse, reminding me to learn
the secrets of the poets who gave me a good return.

But most of all my family, the future is in them,
they never fail to be there when I need them once again;
and I devote my life to making sure that they stay well,
I know my way about this world, their fears I can dispel.

A helping hand, supporting word, my time is precious too,
I give them my attention as I want them to renew;
if I can leave a legacy, I'd teach my kids to share,
have faith and hope in God above and show Him that you care.

My Ocean

My eye is drawn to deepest blue
imbued am I by size;
the ocean hue— a painted view
as skies reflect my eyes;
and when I breathe in fresh sea air
I'm filled with hope
and how to cope;
the foamy soap
has so much scope
I slope to shores to soak— repair.

(The Chime Operandi)

My Loyal Queen

My Queen, my Queen, don't leave me here—
alone without your love and care;
I'll never leave your side, it's clear
you walked into the Devil's lair.

Devoted to the Popish school
you'll die a traitor, this is true;
Elizabethan rule is cruel,
and friendlessness is nothing new.

I hide inside your petticoat
and weep for you my loyal Queen;
my love for you I will devote,
your destiny was unforeseen.

One eyewitness account states that Mary Stuart, on the day of her execution, had a tiny dog that had hidden within the folds of her skirt. Robert Wingfield wrote about it.

His account does not describe the colour or breed of dog, some believe it was white and others say it was black, and the breed was very likely to be a Scottish Terrier. But these facts cannot be verified.

Nature's Battles

The battle starts at birth for some,
so many trials to overcome;
when weather brings the freezing snow,
they fight with predators you know.

The battle can be lost sometimes,
when bravery has crossed the lines;
and death occurs too soon for some
so many trials to overcome.

The battle always comes on strong,
no matter whether right or wrong;
no justice in this world prevails
when hateful deeds have tipped the scales.

The battle in the wild is real,
when others try to rob and steal;
survival means they overcome
the trials outside are fought and won.

Never Alone

There's nothing like
a clear blue sky,
to melt my eye,
and soothe my soul,
and make it whole;
a sunny day can lift me up
in late July,
my mind and body
in control
a stroll beneath the sun,
warm days in good supply.

I dip my toes in salty sea,
on sinking sand,
as waves of foam
help me atone;
and I forget the grief,
as I lay on the land
to face the heat,
although alone
I never feel
I'm on my own,
I touch your hand.

New Chicks for the Eagles

Not every mission has success,
as failures may make us confess;
but if we keep on trying here—
in time we will make chicks appear.

The Eagles are not daunted by
the cloud or snow held in the sky;
their mating will bring forth new life
as these two birds will battle strife . . .

against all odds tenaciously
they will succeed courageously
and in the nest we'll view a babe
to strive with pride in this crusade.

Early in 2022 year Jackie and Shadow, two Eagles in California sat patiently on two eggs that did not hatch. The weather was unusually cold and the eggs did not survive. However we think they may try again as they have been preparing the nest once again. Fingers crossed.

New Home – New Memories

When every home requires a heart to help it beat in time,
infused with love and tenderness a happy home has rhyme;
the melody within its walls will sing with joy each day,
with faith and hope the soul within can wipe a tear away.

As home is where we rest our head, a place we can relax
recuperate, and be inspired, and mend those little cracks;
where smiles uplift, they are a gift, when life is going wrong,
a home is where we're understood, and empathy is strong.

Night Falling

Ring, ring, ring
tolls the old gold bell, in town,
and I am heartened by the clatter
wakening me with its sound.

Sing, sing, sing
from the church, a choir in key—
the voices soothe my soul if only
I could let myself be free.

Tap, tap, tap
slap the drops of rain, outside
that trickle down my window jetting
with a surging tidal ride.

Dark, dark, dark
runs the night time sky at dusk,
as shadows cast foreboding branches,
trees that scare and run amok.

Ring, ring, ring
tolls the old gold bell, in town,
and I am heartened by the clatter
wakening me with its sound.

Night Lights Dancing

The coastal road was strewn with leaves
the sun had kissed the sea—
the rusty chain was squeaking
on my ancient peddle cycle.

Dusk turned down the light
as darkness killed my jubilee
and nothing could prepare my eyes
for scenes against the twilight sky!

A buzzing flash, a yellow glow
quite low and dancing in the air—
a flare of dots came on and off
as something skipping, swaying here
was soaring near persistent pampas.

I stopped to watch the light parade
and they were watching me—
electric fire flies flew by,
they formed a frantic flit and flirt
and on my flowered skirt they danced
then vanished and I could not see.

The show was over, all alone
the squeaking then continued—
and riding home, the clover glowed
with amber spots of beaming light;
how magical is nature when its free!

No Access

No access here, no cheery act—
he sat and watched my tries;
this stupid brat, no eyelid bat!
This fool was no surprise.

When I complained, he stood and sighed,
defied the highway code;
and passers-by would ask him why
he was not on the road?

He drove his car across my route,
this dude just did not care!
In his pursuit, his deed acute
no thoughtfulness was there.

No Boundaries

Beyond the surface of the pond—
the wrongs are rife within;
amid the pong, the smell is strong,
and full of evil sin.

As kin would suffer from the din—
herein wild tempers fly;
beneath the skin, the blood is thin,
so many here would cry . . .

defy me if you dare, he'd sigh . . .
as I will use my sword
and for an eye, I'll let you die,
no boundaries are sworn.

(A Metrical Echo)

No Love to Share

I never heard him say my name,
or call me on the phone, explain,
he didn't even hold my hand,
or walk with me on white hot sand.

And every sunset that he missed
I vowed to keep each one I kissed,
and said goodbye to days that went,
without a loving warm lament.

He left without a word of kind,
internally he'd lost his mind;
the image of him standing there
without a word of love to share.

And after we had spent some time,
recorded memories in rhyme
that's all that's left of what we had,
it leaves me feeling rather sad.

But I can't change a mind that's stuck
without belief in faith and luck—
I simply wanted loving arms
to lose myself inside his charms.

Alas my dreams were never real,
as his true nature did reveal,
that nothing changed this sad recluse,
he always had a good excuse.

Noisy Bells

On Sundays the bells never stop making sound
the ringing is loud, there's no peace to be found.
I wonder if those who live close to the church,
are deafened like birds who fall down off their perch.

I close all my windows and pray for some peace,
but noise from the bells never rock me to sleep;
from eight in the morning, 'til sunset at night,
the clanging of metal dongs with a great might.

The call from the parish reminds us to pray,
encouraging all to remember this day;
on Sunday when we should be doing some good,
the noise from the church is so misunderstood.

Nudist Inspection

The nudist with little protection,
could never control his erection.
The bathers won't care
so little was there—
so nobody raised an objection.

(A Limerick)

Odd Socks

Now every sock I ever own,
is colourful and perky—
and freedom reigns within my home,
all socks are rather quirky.

They love to migrate, separate—
and never like to pair;
I wash them, but they just can't wait
to hide beneath the stair!

I find them hiding under beds,
they love to lie with flowers!
I swear my socks have secret legs,
or maybe special powers?

My drawer is full of old odd socks,
the other ones left home.
The pair I loved had bright red spots
one yearned to be alone!

I tried to discipline one old sock,
but it laughed in my face,
until I kept it in a box,
for it was in disgrace.

And my advice is: buy two pairs—
ensure that this bewitching,
will never catch you unawares
when one old sock goes missing!

Offended by the Truth

The truth is often hard to take
by those who never make mistakes;
and no apology is born—
their greater virtue full of scorn.

A self-promoted man of God,
rules over others with his rod;
no empathy or kindness shown,
rigidity, a heart of stone.

Offended by the truth that's told,
this man speaks like his word is gold;
he learned that no one really changes,
roots are deeply set for ages.

(If only he had learned to see,
that it's okay to disagree;
another view is not so wrong,
accept that we can all be strong.

A humble man is tolerant,
opinions that are moderate;
conduct yourself with faith and grace,
without such anger face to face).

Alas this man has gone too far,
he cannot see beyond the bar;
offended by the truth that's told,
this man speaks like his word is gold.

Old News

Don't dwell on the past,
the future is promising—
what's gone is old news.

One of Those days

The vacuum cleaner won't stand up,
and water lingers with no plug--
the milk is sour, there is no bread,
the internet connection's dead.

The phone alarm did not go off,
I think I may have caught a cough;
no headache pills are left to take,
I'm late, I'm late, this is my fate.

The in-laws are about to call,
I need a paracetamol;
forgot to put the oven on--
the dog escaped, he has now gone.

When everything is going wrong,
and you can't hear a happy song--
discover meditation, sleep,
tomorrow brooms will clean and sweep.

Open Up Your Heart

I met a man with one long yearn
to live a life without concern—
his bubble thick, the glass was strong
an no one ever did him wrong.

One day he met his ideal match
a woman he would want to catch—
but penetrating through her heart
would tear the two of them apart.

As neither of them answered calls
their fortresses had mighty walls—
and so they did not make a start
too much protection round their hearts.

A lesson learned when living life
as there will always be some strife
and not allowing it to churn—
means we will never live and learn.

So open up your heart and soul
remind yourself that every goal
will have a winding path to climb,
so make good use of all your time.

Oreo, the Snow Dog

He romps about and kicks the snow,
he never feels the cold you know;
he's off the lead when in the park,
he's full of spark and likes to bark.

He blends into the snowy scene,
plays hide and seek, there is no green;
he never feels the cold you know,
when everywhere is white with snow.

He hates to get himself too wet,
as this makes him a tad upset.
But he cannot resist the snow,
he never feels the cold you know!

Oscar Wilde tells his Tale

A talent way beyond compare, and plagued by human sin,
the tales and poems that he shared have touched us all within;
a moral sense of right or wrong would shape his life and times,
and punishment was harsh for what the law believed were crimes.

His precious gift recorded when he spent some time in jail,
as human degradation was reported in detail;
as wistfully convicted men would gaze up to the sky,
before the hangman placed the noose around their necks to die.

He questioned every aspect of the human will to kill,
the penalties resulted in a bloody overspill;
the final days of those incarcerated in a cell,
were monitored ensuring that the crown despatched to hell.

His words would chill our bones with fear and open up our hearts,
to understand conditions where a man was torn apart;
like cattle herded into rooms where they would lose the fight,
a scaffold crudely built, but so efficient— killed tonight.

The haunting tale of many men who followed in these steps,
was told in rhyme, the tale complex, to tantalise, perplex;
I read his words and touched by sadness that he felt inside,
in Reading where the men were murdered with no place to hide.

This is a story of Oscar Wilde who spent some time awaiting trial for indecency with men which was illegal then, and punished harshly. He served two years hard labour. He witnessed men being taken from their cells to the scaffold where they hung by the neck until dead. From his cell he wrote:
(The Ballad of Reading Gaol).

Our Deeds Tell a Tale

In deeds we can reveal our true intentions,
we can't disguise an action once it's viewed;
the consequences may provide some tensions—
uncover someone meaningfully shrewd.

We send a message to the world with deeds,
they tell a tale of who we really are—
the pattern renders truth with such a speed
that we can know if good or bad will star.

A subtle gesture may be innocent,
but hiding in the shadows is a scheme;
manipulation could be evident—
as calculated callousness is mean.

The world is just a stage, we are on show,
our actions tell us what we want to know.

In 2007, German Chancellor Angela Merkel had bilateral talks with Putin.
In 1995 Angela Merkel was bitten by a dog and she had a fear of them.
When she met Putin, a Labrador dog came bounding in and sat by Angela
Merkel. This was intended to intimidate her and make her fearful.
Evidently she did not let this bother her.
(A Sonnet)

Own Behaviour

It's hard to own behaviour, and admit we wronged someone,
but laying bare our soul can bring us solace, we become
attuned to how our actions can be damaging and real—
and steps we take to make amends encourage us to heal.

These lessons are not learned by all, some never own their deeds,
and never say they're sorry, never grow from loving seeds.
A sadness that is buried deep destroys the human spirit—
to hide behind a lie can often stunt our growth and limit.

And taking on responsibility will help us see
that everyone can make mistakes, forgiving them is free—
an open heart will show the world that we are worth a smile,
and in return you'll always feel refreshed by every mile.

Owning Our Sins

When sinners try to clean the slate and scrub it with their bleach,
their echo, it will not abate, they have a lot to teach—
forgetting they were sinners once, no mercy do they show,
reformers have an empty heart that's full of ice and snow.

They preach inside a pulpit that is rich with vice and shame
and full of indiscretions that have sullied every name;
no moral code or faith in those who always crossed the line—
a soul with no compassion; understanding— they decline.

I recognise these people as their deeds show colours true,
they mingle in the crowd and they are fooling me and you;
their fake facade is fabricated from fictitious faith—
believing that are righteous and their word will carry weight.

The subtle hints confirming that my doubt has truthful roots—
and those who kick the hornets' nest need big protective boots;
to touch a heart within will take a kind and gentle soul,
not someone so determined here to rule and take control.

I've seen through words as deeds reveal the heart of true conviction,
the souls who never need self-praise, deserve my benediction.
Those open to opinion, who consider other views—
are humble souls, in times of war, deactivate, defuse.

Panto Night

A ruffle of excitement, as we know the show will please,
we take our seat, anticipate the fun of comic tease.
The men, they dress as women, and the women dress as men,
the jumble of emotions are all loosened in this den.

The stage is set to bring a smile with every single joke,
with each release the audience will laugh with other folk.
A rich explosive colour scene of vibrant magic zest,
as characters will come to life, and do their very best.

The crowd participates in some ridiculous suggestions—
as players hide and tantalise with stupid silly questions.
The children love the antics of these gifted souls in flight,
a tale is told upon the stage and we enjoy the night.

Those painted faces sing with joy and some will grieve in sorrow,
as good and evil fight it out to win a new tomorrow—
the actors glide, enjoy the ride as Panto's are good fun,
and I decide to take my child to this year's artful thrum.

Paranoia

More deeply than a thought may creep,
a cheap and silly notion;
begins to seep, awakens sleep
into the mind's wide ocean.

And so it will repeat the flow,
and go from waves, to tide,
until we know the biggest show
of paranoia lied.

We tried, but failed with loving pride
to ride the stormy wave;
we all have cried and deep inside,
the answer's in the slave.

(A Metrical Echo)

Peaceful Negotiation

Strong views can ignite a fight
and cause divided loyalties;
songs that once were sweet and bright
now bring in new anxieties.

Wars that start from acorns, grow
into a complex web of strife;
doors then close, we come to know
that conflict steals, and takes a life.

Compromise can calm, console
allows opinion to be heard;
optimising self-control,
to keep the peace, is much preferred.

(A Rimaric)

People Watching

I'm people watching in the town,
and no one here is looking down;
the weather made them bare their chests
some bodies are way past their best . . .

and from the rear the men look strong
with legs like Bill Sykes, hair quite long;
but when I view them from the front,
their big pot belly bears the brunt.

As drinking, eating to excess,
no woman hides beneath her dress;
her shape reveals indulgent ways,
she curses need to use those stays.

The kids are always on the go,
to scream for more, it's what they know;
as parents always will give in,
and sure enough there is more sin.

And in the park there are a few,
who run for life, to start a new;
they exercise 'cos they are wise,
and leave behind those fatty fries.

My observations serve me well,
I am not here to kiss and tell;
or shame by naming names me-dear,
but health is not a lifestyle here.

Phones are a Curse

My walk along the cobbled stones
where many bones have also trod,
and God is looking down at souls
devices stalk, our life is odd.

Can He forgive our ignorance,
indifference, incessant talk,
we squawk in sad belligerence,
and never see or hear a hawk . . .

or praise the beauty of a bloom,
or hear birds tuneful melody
are we immune to fine perfume,
our phone betrays dexterity.

(A Seasoned Octet)

Pink Ladies

Dressed in feathered pink
tall long-legged ladies wade
graceful flamenco

Pink Roses

My roses grow in unique rows
exposing buds in pink;
and I propose my little nose
will into petals sink.

I think these blooms provide a link—
distinctly filled with charm;
a summer wink of magic ink
infuses me with calm.

Disarming all the woe and harm
alarming scenes in life;
my roses arm me with a psalm
a peaceful end to strife.

(A Metrical Echo)

Plagiarism

The judges made certain assumptions
deliberate with their deductions—
the cheat was forbidden
to keep secrets hidden
his plagiarist work caused disruptions.

(A Limerick)

Poodle Doodles

I like to look my very best, then I can hit the town,
I put my owner to the test, when choosing every gown;
I'm spotted by the crowd as I am famed upon the street
and never bark out loud, as my appearance is too neat

I walk with head held high, I have a skip within my step,
the poodle has a name synonymous with little pet;
from toy to fully grown, we are a sight for weary eyes,
impressive is our style, and we can always take the prize.

When doodles are for poodles, we can show that we are bold,
so smile when we parade the town, as we have won the gold;
we celebrate all animals, pretending just like you—
with haute couture, we're fashionable, wear a great tattoo.

Poor Customer Service

What happened to the helping hand
the happy band of cheerful men?
A penned response about the brand
is from that chap who wrote again.

No cheer or talking on the phone,
rejecting moans, don't want to chat,
they bat complaints just like a stone,
and cannot clear a refund back.

The long awaited resolution,
starts a revolution here;
I fear no proper good solution
same old songs are what I hear.

We cannot action refunds now,
the Covid cow has been too strong,
prolonged the process here somehow,
we have no clan, we chug along.

We'll write when we have staff back in
someone akin to do the scan;
I cannot help, assist, begin
please be polite, we have a plan.

Post War Trauma

Indoctrinated by a world at war,
where every tiny noise kept him alert;
a lapse of concentration meant the whore
would steal his life, as he would be dispersed.
Adrenaline was running through his blood,
he knew his heartbeat needed every breath;
and witnessing his friends fall in the mud,
he knew the enemy could cause his death.

He watched and listened, stepping very light,
and didn't care for bees or pretty flowers;
the birds were singing merrily in flight,
intently he would pray for superpowers,
and when the war was over he survived,
returning home to hugs and many kisses;
how happy was he that his mind had thrived,
although exhausted, thankful for such riches.

And in the light of day all sounds disrupt,
he cowered when a sound became too loud;
his instinct was to hide and take a look,
his gut reaction didn't make him proud.
A car alarm, a firework would scare,
and sleep was broken by a memory,
he wondered if his mind would soon repair,
a cure for his distress, a remedy.

Alas, the soldier never could ignite
the passion that he felt before the war,
as once he entered into such a fight
it left the pain of grief inside his core.
and all our soldiers pay a heavy price
as combat is the hardest expectation;
and we can try to offer our advice—
but nothing stops the constant recollection.

Pour your Heart Out

A poet has a duty to be open and be true--
to show their vulnerability, so that you can see through,
a keyhole glimpse of life, just like a spy, they tell a tale--
to make us see what's happening in fine rhythmic detail.

When writing, never hold onto emotion, let it flow,
to touch the reader with opinion, let your heart bestow--
but if you close the door and hide behind deceitful words,
then you will never reap rewards, or get your just desserts.

So show us who you are, and write your story from the heart,
to let us see your tears of sorrow tearing you apart,
your joyful insight into happiness you have been through,
we want to know your feelings, as we want to see your view.

But if you are disguised behind a mask you cannot burn,
then we will never know your deep and meaningful concern.
All Poets have a duty to reveal their soulful verbs,
without it we are reading mediocre empty words.

Precious Christmas Memories

When looking back at Christmas past,
the days we hold so dear;
so many empty chairs contrast
with happy times we cheer.

The years accumulate with love,
and mark our place in time;
we thank our lucky stars above,
and celebrate our climb.

Reflect with perfect confidence,
this year, make it the best;
a tribute to our providence,
the future is a test.

As every year, our memory
records our progress here—
in present times, our history
becomes a souvenir.

Prickly Holly Bush

Your curly lethal leaves of em'rald green,
protect my garden with a sharp reminder
that if I touch a spiky holly Queen
she'll leave a trail of blood on skin behind her.

This glossy evergreen is everywhere,
a Christmas decoration in the sun;
although she fascinates, we stand and stare,
we know she has the will to prick our thumb.

This ardent bush withstands the snow and ice,
she climbs the fence to show her buried treasure;
and robins to the fruit, they are enticed,
a frozen sweet dessert is such a pleasure.

Still tempted are we by her shiny leaves,
and berries bloody with a red reminder—
that if you touch a spiky holly Queen,
she'll leave a trail of blood on skin behind her.

Pride Before a Fall

Before I tripped and took a fall,
recalling my descent;
my mind would stall, and to the floor,
the trip was never meant . . .

I went down on the cold cement,
repenting with a thud;
that very moment my intent—
to save myself from mud!

My foot was caught, and it was stubbed,
my judgement was misplaced;
and when the blood was in a flood
my pride was then erased.

(A Metrical Echo)

Princess of the Night

She stepped into a room
in dangling earring chandeliers;
a princess of the night,
and no one ever saw her tears.
but everybody stared—
at pretty curves and perfect hair,
her confidence was rife,
she tossed her head without a care.

This beauty was for sale,
and her young body was impaled,
by drugs and pills she took,
and on the men she had availed.
This lily shone so bright,
her painted toes were small and light,
as perfume filled the air,
a flair of ambience took flight.

Her beauty was the best,
although at night she did not rest.
She played the game of love,
she can attest to every test.
you'll never know her thoughts,
as her opinions are not sought.
Her mind is on the prize,
it is not love she wants to court.

Her dreams are not like ours,
she has no faith in men or boys;
whilst eyes reflect like stars,
it is her body she employs.
This life destroys the soul
and she will age before her time,
as money is her king—
and it's her trade that will define.

Private Faith

When we can let our neighbour choose, and rise,
and not decide to start a bloody war;
when he has faith in something we despise--
our faith will soothe our soul and will restore.

To praise integrity in our beliefs,
not fight someone who has a diff'rent view;
but show them that acceptance brings relief
to live and let another still renew.

Religious wars in history have shown,
that faith has strength to conquer mighty seas;
suppression never changes minds who own
a strong and firm foundation in the breeze.

Although belief is strong, I still accept
diversity in faith, and have respect.

(A Sonnet)

Puddles

The puddles full of rain and mud
the thud of wellies splash;
I understood the joy of flood
as kids enjoy the crash!

But thrashing with a water lash
has clashed and left a stain
a muddy flash of dirty trash
upon my leg, a pain!

The rain may wash away the grain,
complaining's just for fools;
if I explain, I might attain—
a child who follows rules.

(A Metrical Echo)

Puffs of Death

He puffs upon a coffin nail,
incarcerated in his jail;
dependent on a fix, a drag,
this habit is so very bad.

His breath is green, his teeth are stained,
his sagging skin with smoke engrained;
yet he is happy in the cloud,
the ashen cancer deathly shroud.

He thinks it's cool, he is a man
of Marlborough, he is a fan;
the fag, it promises to earn
a place of notable concern.

His lungs of coal are black as soot,
the doctor has to take a look;
a diagnosis cut life short,
he gazes at the pack just bought.

And when he leaves, he lights the end,
inhaling deep, he can pretend
that everything will be just fine,
ignoring every single sign.

Raiders of the Snowy Mountain!

The battle will commence, each member has a padded suit—
with helmet on, reflective eyes like bugs, they're in pursuit;
and on the mountain top the only way to reach the ground—
attached to feet are wooden skis that slide when going down.

The slope is steep, they jump and leap, with speed they can impress!
The magic of the ride depends on skilful sweet success;
the snowy thrills that spill into a silky smooth descent,
the rapid surge can stimulate this synchronised event!

These raiders on the snowy mountain slide like bugs on ice,
invaders dot inclines cascading from the peaks and heights;
and when they reach the bottom they repeat the ride once more,
to conquer every mountain is adventure they explore.

Real Detectives

They dedicated every hour to solving heinous crime,
protecting young and old from perpetrators was their line;
and I remember how Policing was old fashioned then,
with no computers, diligence was witnessed in these men.

No crime is ever solved without the evidence in place,
obtaining proof was often hard to verify and trace.
But I can testify to culprits standing in the dock
and they were sentenced by the judges, time against the clock.

And nowadays the proof obtained, supplied by those who suffer,
as victims of such crimes have no defence, the law's a duffer;
with violence unpunished, then it might insight a riot,
assaults on women, on the rise, these men are so defiant.

When thefts are unreported, as the Police have no time,
no wonder we can't walk the streets as there is too much crime.
There is no point in cameras, the victim's in the morgue!
Prevention means a presence on the street should be endorsed.

Rebuffed by Love

When all I have to give you is support,
no riches, gems of value— just myself;
my care, concern and wisdom's never short,
as this is where I keep my precious wealth.

My love will be forever, true and free,
without conditions, I will be your friend;
as all I want is you to be with me,
a bond we'll make together, without end.

Alas, what I can give is not enough,
your heart is closed and you won't let me in;
I tried to earn your love, but your rebuff—
confirmed to me that I will never win.

We said goodbye, my heart was torn apart,
you packed your bags to make a brand new start.

(A Sonnet)

Regrets are Few

If I turned back the mighty clock, and missed out all the pain;
what I withstood, just count the good, removing every stain.

I'd relive every moment then, the summer days we walked;
those special dreams, the fun regimes, so many to report.

I'd focus my attention on the places that we saw;
the moonlit nights, romantic sights, I'd never seen before.

But you were blind to everything, except your private plans;
as you were ruled and I was fooled by selfish unkind hands.

And over time I was inclined to drift away from you;
I saw the future with a suture, sewn with much taboo.

My memories are tainted by a shadow in the sky;
to blot the sun, I saw you run, and now I cannot cry.

My eyes are dry, my tears are spent, so many I have shed,
your selfish whim was such a sin and now to me you're dead.

Reflections

The weeping willow dips her sweeping petticoat
into reflecting water looking back;
and she admires her image— makes a special note,
surviving storms means skies are sometimes black.

On sunny days she bathes beside the water's edge,
appreciating life whilst seasons bless her branches;
all complaints are useless, living is her pledge—
and life goes on and she will take her chances.

As she extends a friendship hand to fellow trees,
supporting them with roots beneath the ground;
there is no penalty in reaching out to please,
foundations here are always firm and sound.

Released from Grief

Tell me not in mournful rhyming
of the times long in the past;
leave my head in peaceful chiming
sleep means I escape the blast.

Leave my soul to taste some healing,
sorrow can consume my mind;
grief can grip us with its reeling
tranquil waters can unwind.

Tell me not that I am falling,
when I need to stand alone;
strengthen me, prevent me crawling
on my knees when I'm at home.

Leave me with a word that's warming,
clouds will clear and sun will shine;
put an end to all this mourning,
let the joy of life define.

Renewed Faith

When sun sets on our faith
and we believe that all is lost—
divided are our thoughts because
we pay a heavy cost . . .

as grief can gnaw away at us,
eroding our desire,
and all our inner passion
falls in a pit of fire.

Regaining confidence can take
us on a lonely journey—
jumping over hurdles often
makes us weak and weary;

but when our strength returns and
we can see the light ahead—
renewed is faith in prayers and hope
to clear our foggy head.

Reputation of a Poet

A poet's reputation rests on wording with a skill,
attention paid to wizardry when inking with their quill;
a talent left unrecognised means ethics may be lost,
for envy can be chilling, as it leaves a little frost.

When voting feel the quality, the gift, the flair, the touch.
Did you feel the impact of a clever worded push?
The metaphors, the metre and the flow of rhyming tunes,
and did they ruffle feathers with a poem full of swoons?

As poetry conveys a message, poets touch a heart,
reveal the truth, unmask a lie, a poet can impart—
and words, when used in perfect rhyme can tantalise or soothe,
delivering emotion with a melody that's smooth.

Respectability

She walked with grace and poise,
her heels and hat increased her height—
behind her fearful eyes
her secret life may
shout her out.

Her virtue was unquestioned in that dress,
and haughtiness can add a touch of rank,
respectability had gravity—
deportment was the key to her success.

With etiquette and modesty
she fooled the waiting crowd
her dignity demurely demonstrated—
Was she a woman of great means
and landed title?
Appearances extremely overrated!

And at the races everyone was trimmed
with finery and lace in their disguises—
she placed her bet and watched the winning horse,
excitement let down every single guard!

She shouted out just like a barroom squiffy—
"Cum on Dover, move yer blooming arse!"

Rhyming Swan Song

To rhyme with words and keep the time
in chiming melody;
a fine design, can bring a shine
and polish with its key.

To free a word will guarantee
a sea of tuneful songs—
we can foresee the jubilee
and try to right the wrongs.

When ponds are graced with purest swans,
we bond with scenes of peace,
the days are long and we respond—
on poetry we feast.

(A Metrical Echo)

Ride of my Life

The carousel, it spun me round
can't touch the ground
the music sounds
the ride
had speed
it dipped
my heart it skipped
white knuckles gripped
I tossed my pride, and just complied.

(The Novenary Reel)

Roaches

They came in hoards, they were insane,
their fame proceeded them;
we killed, no shame, it was in vain,
these creatures we condemn . . .

and when these insects start to trend
they tend to stay and curse;
they will offend as they extend
disease can spread and worse . . .

disbursing these brown shirted jerks
a thirst to kill, adopt;
alerted, as the danger lurks,
these roaches never stop!

(A Metrical Echo)

Rotten Explosion

The old dog could not pass his motion
and farting would cause much commotion;
the smell would compare
to thick rotting air—
pre-empting the final explosion.

(A Limerick)

Running . . .

Stepping, walking, hiking, running!
better move than doing nothing:
nightmare tasking, am I dreaming?
legs are knitting, and machining.

Many miles I have been strumming
up and down the street, I'm coming!
music in my ear is humming,
jumping, rushing, fat-burn, crushing.

Oh my goodness, blood is zooming,
breathless, restless, time consuming,
flowers all around are blooming,
I can't stop my feet from moving!

Rule Britannia

Oh Rule Britannia of Waves
as Britons never shall be slaves;
those haughty tyrants ne'er shall tame—
this land of glory, never shame.
So bring my chariot of fire,
as never shall the fight retire,
Jerusalem is builded here,
the cities shall with commerce steer.

Our freedom gained with truth maintained,
on England's pleasant pastures reigned;
my sword will not sleep in my hand—
on England's green and pleasant land.
Heroic blood of many Knights
kept enemies from cliffs of white,
the safety of our precious shores,
as mighty ships have conquered wars.

Majestically shalt thou rise—
despite the blasts we've heard in skies,
protecting every mammoth oak,
our land will not go up in smoke.
Our fame is ancient as the days
and pride is in our rich displays,
the pageantry of pomp and glory
historic'lly it is our story.

Rhyming Song

To rhyme with words and keep the time
in chiming melody;
a fine design, can bring a shine
and polish with its key.

To free a word will guarantee
a sea of tuneful songs
we can foresee the jubilee
and try to right the wrongs.

When ponds are graced with purest swans,
we bond with scenes of peace
the days are long and we respond—
on poetry we feast.

(A Metrical Echo)

Sad Goodbyes

Misty dawn, I am in mourning,
parting fills my heart with chills;
islands in the south are calling,
begging me to mountain hills.

Hearts are breaking, eyes awaking,
sunshine days will be a phase—
English trees I am forsaking,
icy pavements, frosty rage.

Tear filled eyes and sad good-byeing,
promises with hugs forgive;
picturesque are scenes abiding,
drawn to places where I live.

Spring will chart with its enchanting,
flowers bloom to lift the gloom;
coming home, we'll all be laughing,
happiness will fill the room.

(A Hectic Heptad)

Scoring Goals

This girl of British Soccer fame
is scoring goals to win the game;
opponents watch her every move,
for she can score, she's in the groove.

And when Lucinda joins their team
she flies just like a sunny beam;
and like a stealthy silhouette—
she kicks the ball into the net.

And on the pitch her feet are fast,
her speedy running is a blast;
hurrah they shout, another goal!
As Lucy Lou is in control.

Seeds of War

Surrounded by his sycophants, another man with hate,
has pushed the boundaries and mapped a course to change his fate;
and now he has revealed himself, his colours we all see,
a tyrant with no honour, and the world cannot be free.

Will sanctions change his point of view? Manipulate this deed,
I doubt he thought of consequences, planting seeds that weed;
the rotting flesh on carcasses where vultures flock to feed,
to pick the bones of dead men in this grubby land grab greed.

This power hungry little man has blood upon his hands,
he lied and cheated everyone as he had secret plans;
the world records and knows about deceitful treachery,
repeating in this act of violent cruel butchery.

But every man will ultimately face their judgement day,
excuses will not save them and there will be hell to pay;
their legacy will leave a trail of sorrow and of grief,
there is no turning back the clock for this cold hearted thief.

Serving Time

Be careful what you wish for
when you have the chance to shine.
An open heart and mind to pave
the way to every rhyme.
A course of truth and honesty
will reap the best rewards,
and never draw your sword
just to gain and reap awards.

But if you show true colours
and the dye begins to drain,
then everyone will know that
you did all of it for gain;
and if recruiting others means
you can commit a crime,
you will be all alone—
and left to serve some prison time.

Seventy Years

What happened to all of those years?
The times we drank beers and said cheers;
the fun in the clubs,
the smiles and the hugs,
the boys and relationship tears.

Then busy with babies and schools
and following dietary rules;
feeding and nappies—
Mothers or lackeys?
The pushchairs and bottles were tools.

In the blink of an eye, time flew by,
and our cup seems to be running dry;
for seventy years
we were Musketeers
and the future is in short supply.

And throughout all this time we stayed friends
and I know that your friendship extends—
supportive and kind
you're my lucky find
and your solid advice never ends.

I shall drink to your birthday today,
as this milestone occurs here in May
I wish you the best
our life has been blessed
and I'll send you a flowered bouquet.

For Angela

Shallow Hearts

There's nothing more divisive,
than a flimsy shallow heart,
a fickle emptiness to rot,
and tear the soul apart;
there is no depth of feeling here,
as cold and dark are eyes
and candy smiles are worthless--
as what's left are bitter cries.

Ingenuous are those who
think they know another brother;
without the chance to touch
them deeply like a soulful mother.
And so manipulation
has a feckless wicked face,
a shallow heart will soon dismiss
they're gone without a trace.

And what you thought was real
was just a figment in the mind,
you thought you'd touched their soul,
but they are obstinate, unkind;
and once you learn your lesson,
there can be no turning back,
as someone with no ethics
should be left alone to crack.

Shoe Horned In

I'm shoe horned in from toe to heel,
stiletto reds have much appeal;
I cannot walk as they're too high,
my head now reaches to the sky.

I stand up proudly, tall and chic,
these platform reds are so unique;
my toes are squashed in like sardines,
Louboutin shoes fulfil my dreams.

I sit, cross legged I cannot move,
I know my feet now disapprove;
designer shoes that make me hobble,
stilts cause me to wibble wobble.

A walking stick may help to steady
on the catwalk feeling heady,
suddenly my ankle's weak
I lose the dignity I seek!

I crash and burn, my fall is hard
and on the floor my pride is scarred;
Louboutin heels beyond compare—
have made a scene, as people stare.

Where are my trainers? Send for them!
A place where feet will not condemn
or moan and groan, or feel on fire,
forget Italian desire!

Louboutins I admire, they're neat,
but not so good to wear on feet;
I'm still in awe and passionate,
but they stay in my cabinet.

Shooting Stars Fall

We sailed the oceans, kissed at night,
and watched the light at early dawn;
forlorn, uncertain was your plight,
would tell a tale where I would mourn.

A perfect setting-- sea and sun,
at first the fun was ambient;
my wants, desires I fell upon,
as nothing burred my champion.

Romantic nights beneath the stars,
when string guitars were musical;
the strumming melody disarms--
together tanned and tropical.

Now you are gone, my life at peace,
in this release I can recall,
the fall was never meant for keeps--
but time just flew and built a wall.

(A Seasoned Octet)

Silver Linings

When the pigeon kept stopping in flight
as his pooping had lasted all night.
From trees in the sky
he'd coat passers-by
with some droplets of runny white blight.

Consuming too many rich berries--
his southern trip to the Canaries
postponed for a time,
his health in decline--
and late for his date with the ladies.

Deciding to stay for the winter,
he found that a lonely old spinster
had suffered a dose
she cuddled up close--
they married in famous Westminster.

Inside this short tale there's a moral
a cloud with a lining of sorrow
may turn out okay
at end of each day
have hope for a brand new tomorrow.

(A Quartet of Limericks)

Simple Scenes Inspire

Inspired am I by life's great plan
to see and hear all that I can;
and smell the flowers every day
as life is good in every way.

The optimist will see a world
with stars and moon, expertly pearled;
a sea reflecting skies of blue,
an optimist enjoys the view.

In nature life is always keen
to take advantage of the scene;
an opportunity is there
in trees and forests everywhere.

So take a leaf from nature's book
and go outside and take a look;
there's so much there, and it is free
so be inspired by what you see.

Sleep Well my Love

Sleep my love and think of me,
remember how we danced;
keep that faithful guarantee
a love we shared, romanced.

Lay your head to rest a while,
and dream of long ago;
life we shared, enjoyed the mile
with family we know.

Know we'll miss your kindly face,
unique were all your words,
warm and loving sweet embrace,
we shared our diff'rent worlds.

Missing you at every turn,
but you are near me here;
always showing me concern,
I love you so, my dear.

Smile

A smile can travel many miles,
when radiating through the crowd;
it can beguile when in the light,
we laugh out loud to quell the trials.

We fight against the darkest night,
with hope and faith, we push on through;
to fly our kite, we pray for sun,
a sunny view will then ignite.

So come on let your grin become
your cure when rain begins to fall;
we won't succumb to misery—
when smiles recall the blissful fun.

(The Cryptic Labyrinth)

Snowy the Cat

Snowy the cat was as wide as a mat
so fat that a rat would take over the flat.
Lazy all day, with her idle display—
neglecting her job to keep ratty at bay.

No one would question the Queen on her throne,
she gave out her orders, prestige overblown;
eating too much had resulted in war
her owners were ready to show her the door.

Exercise, dieting fulfilled her dream,
it gave back her confidence, her self-esteem.
Snowy the cat is now trim and so slim,
her patience with ratty is wearing quite thin.

Mistress at home, she is ruling the roost.
her weight loss has given this cat a big boost;
bossing the owners about with her charm,
she's quick off the mark when she hears the alarm.

Social Marketing

Is the world now always crashing,
keep on trashing, people's words!
News is smashing with its thrashing,
storylines with great absurds;
Shocking, mocking with its locking,
making us read every time,
can we break without us cracking
from the loss of friends online.

Liking, typing, wiping, sniping,
jibes that hurt and cut our heart,
why do we keep socialising
on a platform with no chart.
Picking, popping, people stalking,
shadows that remain unseen,
watching, clocking, Huns keep blogging,
gaming, staining, words obscene.

Monitored is all our shopping,
advertising splinters views,
egos are just like mosquitos,
biting, snapping with abuse;
perfect faces, with no braces,
spaces are reserved for you,
targeting you, knowing, growing,
marketing you through and through.

Socialist Control

When banning books of opposition,
brings about suppression,
the government is in remission,
lying with aggression.

This period of telling lies
and fooling everyone,
will end in tears, when someone dies,
the party is undone.

As socialists control the news—
usurping tidal waves;
and those who fight against these views
will soon be in their graves.

Solving Puzzles

Investigators searched high and low
to find the man responsible,
they did not know he was in plain sight--
too blind to see him standing there.

Disguises are clever
when they portray the ordinary--
when everybody is looking
for the extraordinary.

Try too hard
the wool falls over eyes,
impassive idle thoughts
bring imagination to life,
and crimes are solved
facts reveal the truth
and there lies the answer--
it was under our noses all the time.

Just like writing poetry--
let your thoughts roam free
and who knows
where the story will take you,
and what you will discover.

Some Mothers

When Mothering a child, it is for life,
and never does the nurturing abate;
a job that lasts through good times and in strife,
a Mother never cracks beneath the weight.

And when a Mother dies, she leaves behind
a legacy that lives through generations,
and this is why a Mother should be kind--
to foster firm and reinforced foundations.

Not every Mother cares, as some are cold,
the child is scarred by callousness and doubt;
and grows without a loving hand to hold,
without a lasting love that is devout.

This does not mean that others will not see
how much they can be loved by you and me.

(A Sonnet)

Songs Reflect Life

I hear a tuneful melody
the key will start to cheer;
I never fear the memory
and see a picture clear.

The moment when we wed, a song
of love that left me very strong.

Now time has passed and you are gone,
the sun begins to shine;
you left behind a song, the one
upon my heart sublime.

(A Pinned Decimal)

Soulful Music

Soul to soul music
from romantic feathered friends
tweeting messages

Sounds of Love

Displays of sweet affection as these lovers make a vow
when soaring through blue skies they fly in unison somehow;
on fences bowing, petting as this ritual is rife,
as delicately dancing wins the heart of every wife.

The nesting preparations are perfected with great zeal,
and parents know the task ahead will be a big ordeal;
as chicks can be demanding when they're hungry for a life,
with mouths to feed, the challenge can be full of stress and strife.

The dedication to each other, indicates their love,
the pair will stay together and forever fly above;
and mating seasons bring such joy as fledglings find their wings
a song is sung to serenade, at dawn the sound begins.

Speak for those who have no Voice

I speak for those who cannot speak,
those souls who are too weak or meek;
I am the voice of those not strong,
the people who are told they're wrong.
My words can reach up to the stars,
and sing with music from guitars;
my message comes from silent tongues,
informing all to leave their guns.

To think before condemning men,
to understand, and see again;
to open up their hearts and listen,
hear their plight and know their mission.
I speak for those who can't be heard,
because no one received their word;
they have been silenced by the crowd,
and drowned by those who are too loud.

Suppressed by laws that stole their lives,
and no one hears those haunting cries;
as Governments bulldozed a path,
through ashes in the aftermath.
And held to ransom, sold in hell,
the one's who tried to speak and tell;
injustices hide in the wings,
the poet must expose these things.

Spice up our Life

Variety in poetry,
it is the spice of life,
so sing your song with gaiety,
to quell the world of strife;
don't stick to only subjects,
that will bore the pants of us!
Go write a controversial rhyme—
to make a lot of fuss!

Stay Focused

The stirring of some talent lay inside the air like fog
and one who had dislike for it, was like a rabid dog;
intentions were so spiteful, that their deeds were murderous,
they stamped upon this rivalry with avariciousness.

Malicious, speedy words were shot like arrows through the air,
they pierced the hearts of anyone who dared to read and share;
and with this doubt and prejudice the writer died inside,
it stripped him of identity and all his inner pride.

The mortal wound had killed his inspiration for a while,
he never rose from sleep, and he would never walk the mile;
the melancholy lasted for a month or more in time,
and we have learned that jealousy, is such a heinous crime.

So never let a harsh critique dry up the ink of skill,
and rise above a bad review and never let it kill--
exuberance and passion for a story or a poem,
knit together unique words to keep your writing going.

Stay Strong

The joys of life abundantly
will guarantee the good times roll;
the goal will be triumphantly
to praise, rejoice, infuse the soul.

We know misfortune hits us hard,
do not be scarred, or be destroyed;
a noisy life can soon bombard—
don't fall to woe— an empty void.

The balance of a life well lived,
we can forgive, we can forego;
bestow our courage and forbid
our rationale to drown in snow.

(A seasoned Octet)

Stone Cold Love

His love came with some thoughtless words,
conditions hard and stern;
demanding my attention hurts,
affection I must earn.

His insecure, unstable nature—
lends itself to death,
in this I think he has a major
boring, stiff on meth.

Yes he is like a zombie, true,
no humour in his smile;
no jovial or sparkle grew
when he behaved hostile!

His deep green eyes were lacking in
that passion I looked for!
His manner was quite sour within,
to be with him, a chore!

I tried to see the positive,
the dead are stony cold;
he exercised prerogative,
and swiftly died I'm told.

Stop the Gum

The world is full of chewing gum
and chewers are the worst;
they drop the stuff and just a crumb
gets stuck and won't disperse.

The dark black dots are everywhere
the chewers leave behind--
a blob of glue is what they share,
the deed is not refined.

The town is scarred, the street is marred
by chewers who are dotty;
how would they like their own back yard,
to look so grim and grotty.

So take your gum and spit it out
into a dusty bin;
don't leave it in the streets you lout
this is a mortal sin.

It costs around 7 million a year to clean the chewing gum off pavements.

Stubborn

The stubborn minds who never learn,
although they hear quite well,
refusing every time to listen,
heed the metre bell;
they plod along, the same old song
without a tune within—
and yet they have so much to say,
and want to write a rhyme,
but words are out of order
and devoid of any chime.

Sunshine

Rays of cheerful light
direct beams upon the earth
life quenched with grand hope.

Sweet Meat

The meat delivered raw and keen,
now drained of blood, it looks so clean.
Were these poor creatures really dead,
once free to run near flower beds?

Without their heads, so stiff and cold,
they died too soon, did not grow old.
What happened to their feet so neat
chopped up and sold for us to eat?

When will this barbarism end?
Do we need meat to heal and mend?
Can we survive on plants and seeds;
and honey from those buzzing bees?

The dead lined up outside the shop,
not one eye wet, no one was shocked;
we are accustomed to the kill,
to eat lean meat is such a thrill.

So let these words be food for thought,
the butcher never is distraught;
he chops up flesh and bone each day,
as selling mutton pays his way.

Taliban Rule

She lost her soul, she lost her hope,
all freedom is now gone;
the Taliban now beat and choke—
a new life has begun.
They cannot work or drive a car,
the veil of hate descends;
as women bear the dreadful scar—
as men's control offends.

A poor defenceless female now
is beaten half to death;
and watched is every detail how
this punishment has depth.
Courageous is the woman—
her bravery is clear,
and taken to her bosom
is a faith she once held dear.

But now she knows the truth of it
severe and harsh is life;
it's ruled by brutal men who hit
and threaten with a knife.
And under God these men will pay
no Heaven will allow—
the soul of any man to stay,
who took this dreadful vow.

Tears are Shed

Alone my tears are shed inside my solemn head,
another year without the man who shared my bed;
he shared my life, my strife, my inner private thought,
was always there to care, when I was caught, distraught.

I hear his words of comfort bringing eyes to tears,
his wisdom helps me quell all of my anxious fears.
I miss his solid lead, the passion in his deed,
the little things he did, his stoic strength that freed.

The empty place he left inside my heart is strange;
I cannot come to terms with grief, it has no change.
Another year drifts by without a word from him
remembering his kindness, left in me within.

Tears of Joy and Sorrow

There's sparkle in the street where lights are bright
and tinsel glints, reflecting lots of joy;
I hear the choir with carols sung at night,
with children praying for their fav'rite toy.

As Christmas leaves some magic in our hearts,
we celebrate and wrap up those surprises;
and food and drink fill up our shopping carts,
at Christmas we will make some compromises.

But spare a thought for those who are at war,
no cheer, no beer, no festive fun this year,
as bullets filled with hate are at the core,
and tears of sorrow fall, war is severe.

Our prayers will reach all those who suffer now,
and quell their pain with faith and hope somehow.

(A Sonnet)

Tempted by Love

When physical attraction has the power to delight,
the heart is sworn to loyalty, the moment brings a light;
and when it is confirmed, there is romance inside the room—
a look, a wink a smile exudes invisible perfume.

A thrilling atmospheric elevates two doves above,
the subtle process happens when two hearts begin to love;
before we realise it, we have lost our self-control,
and everything's personified when we are on a stroll.

The tingle of euphoria when mind and flesh are one,
a tactile turbulence that peaks within the guise of fun;
and every touch is heightened when it's in between the sheets,
the magic of the moment, when our passion counts the beats.

As love matures with many setting suns and phasing moons,
the union here is tied with happy nights and afternoons;
Our love is silent, filled with gold, and something we behold,
inside our world it means we have a heart and hand to hold.

Terror in the Skies

A dreamy holiday with sun in Disneyworld was sought
excitement pumped inside our hearts, we flew to our resort.
The swimming under bluer skies, so very wonderful
then suddenly our life had changed, 'twas not so colourful.

We watched in horror as they fell, the towers one by one,
and knew that nothing ever could be viewed the same again.
Our holiday cut short, we had to fly back home, but how?
The airports closed, as hearts were froze, we could not move for now.

The chaos that ensued meant flights were cancelled going back,
the airlines felt the skies were under terrorist attack.
The only flight available was one into New York
then fly to France, and organise a flight, instead of walk!

Approaching New York City which was burning from the ground,
a shocking scene from in the air, the silence was profound;
the tearful swell, it was a hell, and many died that day,
and here we were inside this time, and all we did was pray.

Our plane took off across the pond to France where we could board
a flight back home but what we saw could never be ignored;
the devastation of this crime has rippled through the world,
how cowardly this terror is, of how the good are spurned.

Terror Invasion

The voice of reason was not heard,
absurdly deaf by choice;
with no rejoicing bombs had blurred—
interred the concrete joists.

The rubble where a building stood,
left memories of neighbourhood;

And former dwellers watch their homes—
in stony terror storms;
and armies swarm among the bones,
in drones they bring reforms.

(A Pinned Decimal)

The Canterville Ghost

There goes the ghost, I tip my hat,
I'm not a bit surprised by that;
I bought the house with spirits in
and now they're making such a din.

But I'm not scared, they mean no harm,
in fact this ghost has graceful charm;
I think I'll turn the tables here,
and scare them with my gun and spear!

If you insist on midnight haunts,
and acrobatic somersaults--
you really must oil up those chains,
they clang and squeak like ancient trains.

You might have horrified the Brits,
but I'm not fooled by dirty tricks;
across the pond we've seen it all--
you're just another ghost on call.

Eventually you will tire,
and give up on your ghostly hire;
a lively battle might just tame
enthusiasm for the game.

This is a synopsis of a story by Oscar Wilde called The Canterville Ghost.

A wealthy American Minister buys Canterville Chase from Lord Canterville himself with the knowledge that it came with a ghost. The family move in and are not fazed by the ghost, in fact they tease it until the ghost is exhausted and sad. I have not included the ending as I thought this might encourage everyone to read this very short story. It is entertaining, humorous and a joy to read and will only take you an hour of your time.

The City of London

A private world of finance in the city
a secretive society lives here—
this powerful and influential treaty
is full of wealth, prosperity and fear.

The dirty dealers and some criminals,
who earn from people's dying misery—
accumulate their wealth, take prisoners
a fake facade behind delivery.

Avoiding taxes here is guaranteed,
no laws will govern them inside this place;
they hide in offshore countries, money's freed—
supporting firms where they cannot be traced.

The old boys network lives, they hold the keys—
to global cities here and overseas.

The City of London is an historic financial district, home to both the Stock Exchange and the Bank of England and a separate entity to the rest of London and the UK. They have their own laws.

It has its own special status: it has its own government, its own mayor and its own independent police force. The Mayor of London has significantly more political power. The City is home to the Bank of England and has traditionally been considered the financial heart of the UK. The City of London dates back to the Roman settlement of Londinium, which was formed roughly two thousand years ago on the northern bank of the River Thames inside one square mile.

It has been criticised for money laundering and providing tax havens for unscrupulous organisations and the extremely wealthy.
(A Sonnet)

The Crown

A series captured on the screen by Netflix
promoting our great Monarchy for good;
and in this fabrication, are synthetics,
the truth of it is hidden under wood.

Emotional, dramatic-- it appeals,
to all those U.S. hearts who love the Royals,
but I can tell a diff'rent tale that's real,
this institution will protect its jewels.

A stony, stoic core exists within,
where no emotion has a chance to breathe,
there are no tears of joy or sorrow in
this family that's ruled by Royal creed.

The rules will rarely bend, steeped in tradition,
believing they are all above suspicion.

(A Sonnet)

The Fishing Trawler

The birds know where their bread is buttered,
trawlers catch the fish for them;
the skies with wings seem dense and cluttered,
following those fishermen.

The nets are full of fish all squirming
caught inside the trap of hell;
the rubber aprons are disturbing—
sea to boat the fishes dwell.

The chain continues, fish to table
every man needs food to eat;
The Trawlers work, and they enable
tuna, salmon, prawns a heat.

The Great Unwashed

I go about my business, and the street is wet and drab,
and rubbing shoulders with the local folk, I'll have a stab,
as some of them have not been near a bar of soap for years—
the smell intoxicates with fumes that fill my eyes with tears.

I'm in a shop confined with doors and windows tightly shut,
a stinky Herbert stands too near, the air's so thickly cut—
before too long the shop has cleared and he remains inside,
why can't he take a bath sometime, why does he have no pride?

The Great unwashed are not that poor, they just don't give a monkeys,
as washing is a chore that they would rather give to flunkies.
These dirty buggers think polluting with their noxious ways,
is perfectly acceptable, their putrid smell decays.

The pong, it lingers through the air, repulsive to our noses,
contaminates the atmosphere and kills our bed of roses;
so steer well clear of dirty folk, who will not wash themselves—
and circumvent and don't relent, not keeping clean repels.

The King is Crowned

The king is crowned, he waited so long for this day to come,
he spent his life in waiting and today the crown is won;
the Nation celebrates with parties everywhere you go,
and patriotic flags adorn the cities, don't you know.

As Charlie makes some history, his Queen is by his side,
the fond and vivid memories will fill all of us with pride,
and as the country celebrates, we toast to King and Queen,
a holiday regenerates the Royal keen machine.

The Kiss I Miss

What I miss is every kiss,
the bliss of touch I really miss—
such is life, the strife is rife
as kissing I cannot invite.

Every moment we have shared
I dared to memorise you cared;
gone is all I knew before,
remembering is shown the door.

Sitting here in silence dear
I cheer a life that isn't clear;
feeling you inside my dreams,
interrupts my silly schemes.

Memories of your sweet smile,
will always shorten every mile,
what I really missis this—
your loving peck, that little kiss.

The Lady Drank too Much

The lady here drank far too much,
she tripped and now looks out of touch,
displaying knickers in the air,
for all the world to stare and share;

The lady stinks of too much beer,
her hair once perfect, now austere,
her eyes are glazed, she's in a haze,
a tramp upon this worldly stage.

The lady is no more attractive,
drink has made her interactive
sharing thoughts that should be silent,
she's aggressive and she's vi'lent.

The lady has no moral code,
she slips into a slinky mode,
men are watching, they are plotting,
what they're thinking could be shocking.

The lady should know better,
once a fine trendsetter,
drinking too much alcohol,
changes her into a moll.

The lady is now in the gutter,
drunk, as all her words now stutter
cannot walk and cannot talk—
she's all alone without support.

The lady here is just a girl,
misguided as the drink disturbs,
and in that moment all is lost
as she will pay a heavy cost.

The Laws of Nature

The laws of life are never written down,
and nature will demand we pay attention;
and when we're lost, we hope that we are found,
the ups and downs of life are our invention.

We cannot take without some recompense,
a price is paid for everything we earn;
we give our time and cannot fight against
rewarding those deserving when they learn.

And if we hate, not love, we gather sorrow,
and there will be a penalty to pay;
as it may even shorten our tomorrow,
or darken all our sunshine through the day.

Our attitude and gratitude transcend,
and on our close attention they depend.

(A Sonnet)

The Marching Band

I heard the crash of cymbals and I had to take a look,
a drumming thud then pounded like the earth had just been shook,
and in between I heard the tapping shoes in unison
the steps of faithful Christians had only just begun.

It's then I heard a trumpet burst the wind with brassy trigger,
that pierced the air and rang between both ears with noisy vigour.
The oomph of sliding wails came from a trombone on the run,
excited me as I know that brass bands can be great fun.

The French horn and the cornet both have subtle loving notes,
filled the band with magic as they marched and won some votes,
and toes were tapping, voices sang, the public loved the show,
a marching band can lift the heart and spirit— don't you know.

A crowd had gathered in the street to witness moving sound,
and then I heard a tuba trump a new beat it had found.
The blast of brass and drums had livened up the sleepy town,
reminding us to give our surplus pennies to the crown.

The melody of saints go marching into silent streets
and life around had taken on some jolly tuneful beats.
Just like the real pied piper, crowds of people followed on,
the band of happy music-makers carried with them song—

and drifting in the distance went the dying thumps and bellows,
the uniformed salvations were a bunch of happy fellows,
and cymbals lingered on the breeze like crickets in midsummer—
the final sound repeating was the dedicated drummer.

*The Salvation Army brass band is a brass band affiliated with a Corps,
Division or Territory of the Salvation Army. In society, a Salvation Army
band playing in public places during Christian events in the calendar such as
Christmas has become a part of seasonal customs, particularly in the UK.
These soldiers of Christ can be seen at many events throughout Britain and
they are talented musicians. I wanted to promote the work of the Salvation
army through the faith contest as they have a mission based on faith in Jesus
Christ. Their work includes searching for people who have gone missing.*

The Monster Never Really Sleeps

The monster unannounced,
now ready, it will pounce.
And when it wakes,
it bleats just like a sheep--
no longer will we sleep,
but wide eyed, we're alive,
and full of deep resentment
for machines that steal and creep.

This metal hunk knows how to haunt,
and finely tuned by human kind--
to taunt the crowd,
the sound is loud--
it deafens every soul
until we beg it to go underground!

But no one will object, because--
we want to know that this machine
will not be keen
to run us down,
so we will let it bleep a sound.

But when it bleeps in constancy--
me-thinks it is conspiracy
as robots might take charge of us!
And we will not make any fuss--
because we think we're in control
but wait-- machines are just a tool,
so why do we put up with noise,
we have a choice to shut them down,
before we mortals drown
in sounds repeating in
on our farms and towns.

The Parson's Wife

Her husband is the caretaker of souls,
and she will herd the sheep into their pews,
as both are servants with their diff'rent roles,
but she obeys and never can refuse.

The congregation sing and pray to God
bespattered are they with the blood of sin;
the Parson guides with his approving nod,
but she knows what is going on within.

And on the surface everybody smiles,
despite the little secrets that they keep;
the solidarity of loyal wives—
reality of life is rather cheap.

The Parson's wife is confident and true,
but she will take those secrets to the grave;
she leaves a message inside every pew,
her door is open, she is very brave.

She lets the Parson think he's saved them all,
behind the scenes, she is the one at work,
deceit and treachery has marked the wall,
where horror hides and demons always lurk.

And no one can be saved without the truth,
hypocrisy exists inside the church;
so ask the Parson's wife, she sees abuse,
it's visible— she didn't have to search.

The Path to Recovery

Fear not the path of healing,
as it is the road to health;
to quell the stress and gain the strength,
to feed upon our wealth.
The tiny steps to betterment,
are littered with some bumps,
but looking back we see success,
in all our little jumps.

The knocks we take in life can be,
a trial and a curse,
collecting scars, be proud that you
have power in your purse.
The battle will be over and
the future's looking bright,
remembering that others have
a similar plight to fight.

We judge our world inside us with
a narrow minded view,
and often we misunderstand,
and feel a little blue;
unlock your heart with love and faith,
and fill your soul with joy,
and overlook the little things
that sometimes can annoy.

The Picnic

We gathered underneath the tree
my Mum, my Aunt and little me;
for sandwiches and cakes for all
a moment long ago— recall . . .
when days would last for hours and hours
we never minded rainy showers—
playing on the field 'til late
the endless summer days were great.

When Autumn leaves began to shed,
and we were early into bed;
I yearned for picnics in the park
but days grew short with early dark.
In winter when the snow was deep
we'd hear the mouse, his tiny feet
escape the freezing cold outside,
inside our home he would reside.

When spring arrived with yellow daffs
we'd decorate some eggs with crafts,
and painted faces full of cheer,
as Easter meant the warmth was near.
The picnic basket was in use
on sunny days we'd introduce
the cakes and naughty finger food—
that helped to cheer our sombre mood.

The Piper

The piper entertains the crowd,
his talent helps to clear the cloud
his music touched my heart with love
a talent sent from up above.

My day it changed into a song,
the rain and cold no longer strong;
the sun it shone inside my soul
the piper had complete control.

The music brought such cheer to me
ignored by some who could not see;
as what I heard had changed my view,
the sky woke up and turned to blue.

The Railway Station

A keen vignette of human life
the air, a buzzing flack—
the click and clack of suit cases
move forward and move back.
The silence of the digital
mean voices can't be heard—
but rushing, crushing bodies move
a vision almost blurred.

A plastic coffee cup abandoned
on a metal table;
the cold foreboding fake facade
where judgement seems unstable.
Then automatic doors invite
the passengers on board;
performers, beggars, cap in hand
on rostrums are ignored.

A stream of avid travellers
step off the platform edge,
as metal tube-like carriers
move smoothly, like a sledge.
When most of us are fast asleep
the station is awake;
pulsating with activity,
it never takes a break.

The Right to Choose

America has lost its way,
as women have no rights today—
and what about those who are gay
will laws now change to make them pay?

Controlling men are now accused
of bullying, they now abuse
and women are still being used,
and have no basic right to choose.

No man can truly understand
or care to give the upper-hand;
their right to choose has now been banned—
democracy is dead and damned.

The Road Ahead

The winding path lay forked ahead,
excitement filled my heart and head,
would fate be good and let me shine--
be good or bad, the choice was mine.

I stepped beyond the road I knew,
no skill required to forge right through--
not looking back, I made my way,
and left behind a cloudy day.

I took each day and lived it well,
the ups and downs, the sad farewell;
I don't regret a moment here,
I saw, I felt, I heard the cheer.

And spent my time with those I love,
appreciated every dove;
and when the road forks into two--
instinctively, I forge right through.

It matters not which path you take
as attitude will make or break;
our heart will know just how to choose--
we cannot walk in other shoes.

The Salon Trip

The clippers cut and took a snip
then dripping hair was dried;
a salon trip I never skip—
a treat that's not denied.

Inside I'm pampered, I decide,
to find a style that suits;
and then she dyed my crowning pride
the process caused disputes!

The roots turned green and I deduced,
excuses, weak and bland;
she introduced some orange juice
to make it look more tanned!

I planned to make them understand
the brand they used was wrong;
and had been banned from every land,
because the dye was strong!

The Scold's Bridle

For centuries the suffering of women has been seen,
humiliation, torture and the flogging has been keen;
but nothing tops the bridle that was made of solid iron
and worn by those poor souls who tried to fight just like a lion.

The muzzle worn upon the head would press upon the tongue,
a spike compressed, bled on the face, they did not think it wrong;
the pain and anguish terrible, traumatic for the wearer,
submitting to her husband's will, his bidding and his terror.

Preventing speech, humiliation did not end with this,
she wore a leash around her neck, was dragged, and never kissed;
and often from infection, with poor hygiene, they would die,
and no one doubted cruelty, or asked the question, 'why?'

The punishment was used by men against a feeble woman,
and if she disobeyed him, she was sentenced to this prison;
today this is illegal, but aggression still exists,
we'll never live in harmony whilst cruelty persists.

The scolds bridle, witches bridle or brands bridle was an instrument of punishment during the sixteenth century. It was a head muzzle made of a cast iron framework with a tongue piece with a spike attached that was pressed down onto the tongue to prevent speech. It was designed to silence the wearer into submission, and it was also a form of humiliation.

The scolds bridle was used mainly on women at the request of her husband, or family members, because they were too outspoken. The side effects were very unpleasant, painful and sometimes fatal. The wearer would often be led around the town by a leash with a bell around their neck to draw the attention of the crowd.

Cruelty behind closed doors still exists and women are too ashamed and frightened to do anything about it.

The Skye Boat Song

The keys to rule an English throne, lie deep within religion,
with Henry Tudor, seeds were sown, and freedom brought division.
No catholic would take the seat, that many tried to win,
and so the bonnie Prince defeat was full of death and sin.

The Jacobite's revolted, but they did not gain control,
the Scottish fight did not corrupt, the British crown their goal;
and Charlie fled, disguised in dresses, fit for serving gals,
he fled to Skye from his suppressors, quit his trait'rous plans.

And so the Skye Boat Song was born, we hear those tuneful tears,
the bonnie lad from Scotland torn, reliant on his prayers;
and never will the crown belong to Stuart clans again,
as history was sworn to song, this plight of Kings and men.

The Skye Boat Song is a late 19th-century Scottish song recalling the journey of Prince Charles Edward Stuart, also known as Bonnie Prince Charlie from Benbecula to the Isle of Skye as he fled from Government troops after his defeat at the Battle of Culloden in 1746. Sir Harold Bolton, 2nd Baronet composed the lyrics in the 1870s and the line (Over the Sea to Skye) is now a familiar phrase in the tourism industry on the Isle of Skye.

The above poem tells of the history behind this story.

The Spirit of a House

The spirit of a house is all about who's living there,
as corners fill with precious moments that we come to share;
the placement of a picture, or a vase of pretty flowers
they bring to life a silent room, and quell the rain and showers.

The baking smells that fill the memory with tastes of old,
the blankets, and the open fire that keeps out all the cold;
the summer sun that streams through open windows are inviting,
and drinks upon the terrace mark a date that was exciting.

Repeated is routine that stains our heart with happy greets,
the coming and the going, and the sad goodbye that cheats;
the problems that arose, and the solutions that were found,
are soaked within the walls, their meaning has become profound.

As now the house is empty and we swim through memories,
we feel the tingle of a spirit once so wild and free;
and now the vacant house has turned into a dormant shell,
until another family has brand new tales to tell.

The Squirrel

The
squirrel
has hidden
nuts in the ground
endeavours profound
as his digging astounds.
When the snow falls succinctly
his treasures are thickly disguised
when resolve is confirmed, he can find!

(A Nonet)

The Water Park

The rapid ride along the water chute
when bouncing on an air-filled rubber b'lloon
excites the kids along the bumpy route,
upon this wet and cloudy afternoon.

The water park is wild with running water,
as heads bob up and down upon the wave,
a place where minutes seem to be cut shorter,
when fun makes time recede for every brave.

When floating on inflatables outside,
some shrieks and screams of fun are heard by all;
the tossing, turning tantalising ride--
upon this feisty, gusty man-made squall.

As racing hearts provoke the elements--
on scary, speedy, water regiments.

(A Sonnet)

The Widow

The window orphaned by her husband's death,
imprisoned by the dark eternal night,
supported him until his final breath.

She stands beside his grave where she has wept,
and wears her dress of black, there is no light.
The widow orphaned by her husband's death.

The grief has stained her heart much like Macbeth,
succumbing to defeat there is no fight—
supported him until his final breath.

And sapped is all her power, and her strength,
she prays that very soon the two unite.
The widow orphaned by her husband's death.

Yet courage will infuse and intercept,
she did her best, and memories are bright,
supported him until his final breath.

The glass will now reflect a life of depth,
with riches deep within, about her knight.
The widow orphaned by her husband's death,
supported him until his final breath.

(A Villanelle)

322

The Worm has Turned

The squirming big fat wriggly worm
would rather earth was not so firm,
as he can't crawl beneath the soil
and in the sun he just might boil.

Exposed is he to all the birds,
and being eaten thus disturbs;
he's fodder to the fishermen
who hook and sink, when he can't swim.

An apple fell upon the ground
and here a home the worm had found;
he crawled right in to hide himself—
and ate his way through all that wealth.

The worm will damage all the fruit
intention is to eat, pollute;
he used his skill, he's unconcerned
and fighting back, the worm has turned.

They did not Shout

They did not smile, they did not shout
just stunned into a silent clout;
to see such stark humanity
be face to face with this account.

How did we sink as low as this?
The cruelty of knuckled fists—
the depths of deep depravity,
where human frailty exists.

Those bullied men succumb to death
and taken was their final breath—
this world produced insanity,
and where is pity in this quest?

Thinking Too Much

When thinking of all things that may disrupt,
and concentrating on the fear ahead;
I realise in life we may distrust—
as wisdom makes a cautious mind feel dead.

As liberty no longer has a say,
controlled within the prison of our mind;
our view is sullied by a cloudy day,
and even when the sun begins to shine . . .

the gloom of what might happen starts to form,
and possibilities begin to seed—
but what if this, or that, what if a storm
then opens heavens for a weed to feed.

If life is threatened, we can always run,
though fearing the unknown is wasting life;
so save your energy for times that come,
as living in the moment kills the strife.

As some souls fear the future and the past,
and whether it is good or bad we learn,
a precious moment's never built to last
forever forward facing, time will burn.

So live each minute given, it's a gift,
and pity those who miss out on the gems;
our time on earth is oh so very swift,
we should be using time to make more friends.

Thoughts of a Poet

From birth, this little babe in arms,
this child with force, would set alarms;
and touched by words, rebuffed absurds,
she knew veracity disturbs.

She vowed to open up and touch,
escape that strangle holding clutch;
to be set free from all restraint,
the borders she would fight against.

Reveal the secrets held by those
abusers whom we all oppose;
and spread the word in poetry
to gain some notoriety.

Expose and taunt those men in power
and bring some justice to the hour;
to turn the tide, and with some pride
tell tales of those who laughed and cried.

Appreciate and dedicate,
encourage those who drown in hate
to change their drastic point of view,
infuse their spirit and renew.

Give hope when all is lost and gone,
embrace a simple golden sun;
and teach the world to share their smiles,
with bravery, to face life's trials.

And when she laid her head to rest,
then she can say, she did her best;
a difference, albeit small--
that left her feeling ten feet tall.

Thrift is a Gift

She's profligate with funds in an attempt to lift her mood,
her spending spree just made all matters worse;
the credit card declined, no money left for fam'ly food,
reflecting on her very empty purse.

Her spiralling depression meant she lost her way in life,
now begging for forgiveness for her sins;
we blame ourselves, succumbing to the advertising strife
the retailers, the trickery, our whims.

The debt continues as the wanting, yearning for solutions
brings her to her knees, temptation real;
and searching for an answer, she will seek those resolutions,
as finances can be a big ordeal

And thrift is underrated, yet it liberates the soul,
the saving of a penny can result
in saving up a fortune, every time we reach our goal,
a thrifty life is easy to construct.

Thugs

Forceful are the words and deeds
a bully bleeds us dry, but why?
Coarse and cruel he wants those leads
to gain position, he will try.

Jealousy will prompt his hand
to violently control someone;
legacies of his command
where he has scored, and he has won.

Stand your ground and have a plan
to cunningly observe his life;
land your big surprising scam
subjecting him to equal strife.

Time

We use it, waste it, try and liberate it,
but time slips through our fingers when asleep;
we curse it, love it, submit our heart and soul to it
and never can we hold it when it leaps.

Timothy Evans was Innocent

A cap of black when death is served,
as murder here, a crime observed—
the judge passed sentence on that day
for killing, he would have to pay.
A simple man, low self-esteem,
the prosecution thought him mean;
assumptions made were very wrong,
his life would not last very long.

He shouted out that Christie was
the man who killed his wife because
he had the opportunity—
he pleaded for immunity!
They strung him up, the deed was done,
a guilty verdict here was won—
and Evans lost his life this time—
he was not guilty of this crime.

As Christie had a killing spree—
he raped and murdered more you see;
in total eight dead bodies found,
prolific killing was profound.
And Evans lost his wife and child,
and died when bias was applied,
convicted wrongly, blood was spilt,
injustice in the court with guilt.

Timothy Evans was convicted of killing his wife and child and was hung on 9th March 1950. The truth was revealed when the bodies of 8 people were discovered buried in the garden of 10 Rillington Place, the home of John Christie.

John Christie was arrested and confessed to the murders. He was subsequently hanged on 15th July 1953 at HM Prison Pentonville. After he was held down for execution, Christie complained that his nose itched.

In January 2003, the Home Office awarded the relatives of Timothy Evans ex gratia payments as compensation for this miscarriage of Justice. In 2004 the conviction was quashed and Evans was granted a pardon for the conviction of killing his wife and daughter, and declared him innocent of these crimes.

To the Gallows

They had no words, no speech was made,
no dying wish, remorseful trade;
as they believed their work was true
no mercy shown, it was taboo.

Brutality spoke volumes here,
as many men would volunteer
to execute and shoot them dead,
a bullet travelled through each head.

The pit where many fell inside
no prayers were said with Genocide;
together buried in a heap,
no one was left to mourn and weep.

The systematic killing reigned,
distasteful loathing had remained;
the graves of souls now haunt the land,
as death for thousands had been planned;

_ _ _ _ _***_ _ _ _

Arrested for the crimes committed
none of them would be acquitted
sentencing was quick and swift,
the hangman's noose became a gift.

They stand to face their Maker now,
the judge had forged a solemn vow;
for murder was a heinous crime—
so many died before their time.

Their guilt was not in any doubt
the punishment was meted out;
the rope was tight around each neck
they fell right through the open deck.

The instigators were severe,
revenge was not the reason here—
humanity demands respect,
and death by hanging was correct.

Tommy Shelby

Oh Tommy how you charm the ladies with your sexy eyes--
your ripened lips could moisten in between a woman's thighs;
commanding is your Brummie voice that thrills with every note,
so piercing are those deep blue eyes, that always wins our vote.

Inhaling on that cigarette with toxic chills inside--
that leaves a trace of danger that invites a flushing tide;
a carnal lust arising from a look of sensual power,
that whispers in erotic words ensuring there's a shower.

The quiet confidence you own will peel away our clothes
intoxicated are we as your body is exposed,
and all resolve has melted as we fall into your arms,
with hope the earth will move, and we are taken to the stars.

Touch our Hearts with Good Deeds

Touch my heart with tender words,
and move my spirit with your caring eyes;
give devotion like the birds,
to dry my grief-filled tearful crying skies.

Open, friendly, loving arms,
that hail the honest brotherhood of man;
seek some peace without alarms—
as war insists on taunting with its plan.

Praise the fight to keep us free,
against the tyrant wielding sharpened swords;
peace has little guarantee,
and warring words have terrifying chords.

Touch our hearts with kinder deeds,
and move the crowd with spiritual acts;
give to those with faithful needs,
to end the crisis, stop futile attacks.

Toxic Bar

The bar is full of hopeless souls inside
who drown their troubles in a deadly mix,
they drink elixir made of sweet surprise—
the brain is numbed by alcohol— the fix.

Great aspirations die among the throng,
there's no tomorrow in a place like this;
it dies in every single drinking song—
the night is young and love is in a kiss.

The stupor takes effect in fantasy
a world where life is full of happiness,
the eyes are blurred, this is insanity,
the body still remains in sleeplessness.

The morning brings a cold wind at the door,
reality is banging on the head—
those troubles are still gnawing at the core,
survival means the pain is never dead.

The cycle then repeats until the soul
is pickled in a toxic liquid tar—
and when the day is done, there is a goal
to head towards the nearest local bar.

Trapped

I'm trapped inside this poem,
and it will not let me out!
The words have blocked my exit,
and I've tried to scream and shout.
Now Sleep is not an option as,
There's ringing in my ears--
the verbs and metaphors are loud,
and bringing me to tears.

I'm in a darkened room,
and all the walls have blocked my light,
some thought of war and death is real,
perpetual the night.
So how can I release my head,
from rhythmic dancing words?
They're taunting me with rhythm,
and my pen flies like the birds.

I'm begging here to be released,
the poem has the key;
until it is completed,
then it will not let me be!
Then suddenly an extra word,
the poem's in good shape
to open up the doorway--
and I can finally escape.

True Friendship

I truly know what friendship is,
the proof is evidenced
in deeds, not words, we often miss
with faithful providence.

Austere hard facts are stark and cold
as we negate the truth,
and sometimes we need someone bold
to guide us like a youth.

When love can blind our eyes from life
and steer us to the brink,
we need a friend who knows of strife
with words to make us think.

To offer their advice in kind
without reward or payment;
a friend who helps make up our mind,
a fine two way arrangement.

Trumped Up

The Trump haters gather like mobsters in black
they never relent from their fatal attack.
To maim and to kill every positive vibe,
accusing and prodding and saying he lied.

The victim is strong, with a powerful smile,
his lawyers are line up to go for the mile,
success will depend on the battle ahead—
until the Trump haters confirm that he's dead.

I wonder is it really happening here?
The land of the free? Do we all need to fear?
Oppression, maltreatment and torture abound,
harassment and punishment beats to the ground.

As history shows that some leaders have lied
and continued in office despite the divide,
yet none of them suffered from such an assault
as Trump has been exiled for being so blunt.

I fear for America losing its way
performances played out in public today,
the world has been watching this victimisation,
the trumped up debacle of each allegation.

Truth Prevails

The innocent were maimed and killed by cowards of the night,
who planted bombs with nails and things to injure and cause strife;
November twenty-first would be a time I'd not forget
whilst drinking with some loyal friends, our lives were under threat.

The IRA would leave their mark on Birmingham forever,
by killing, harming with a bomb, they maimed with their endeavour;
and twenty-one poor souls then died, the shock brought me a chill
by luck I was at home that night, and me they did not kill!

The terror, it continued as the British suffered losses,
these terrorists killed royalty, we buried them with crosses;
You could not see these cowards as they hid their ugly faces,
and everywhere they went they left a trail of death in places.

The Northern Irish people who were British citizens,
protected by the army, they were faithful Protestants;
and lived in fear of Catholics, insisting they had rights
to kill and gain control of Northern Ireland overnight.

And I remember those dark days, they struck our children down,
when innocently drinking in a pub in my home town;
forgiving is not easy when there are so many losses,
and burying the young who were the victims of these tossers.

Tuneful Mornings

The birds have learned to rise at dawn,
they're sworn to find the words,
their sweet returns awake the morn,
performance here affirms . . .

that song is how the birds relate,
there is no argument, debate . . .

the twittering has purpose here,
their cheer is full of praise;
as it conveys that love's sincere,
endearing cabarets.

(A Pinned Decimal)

Turkeys Escaped Thanksgiving!

The turkeys thought that it was time to party,
as they all know their backsides will soon fry;
they love their rum and coke, cocktail Bacardi,
you never know, it might help them to fly!

So having fun was what they all decided,
tomorrow they would raise some hell on earth;
a night out on the tiles got them excited—
they hit the town, the rest was somewhat blurred.

The roof top bar provided atmospherics
they diced with death when tempting providence;
until they all took flight whilst in hysterics,
and glided in the air to Paris-France.

The French don't celebrate when it's thanksgiving!
The turkeys lived their days out reminiscing.

(A Sonnet)

Turkey or Pork

The turkeys lined up for the stunt
today they'd show their zeal;
refusing food meant they could confront—
now slim, they would reveal.

The runway clear for their escape,
now primed, and going steady;
they're fit and healthy, tip top shape,
not dead and oven ready.

The boys brigade took to the skies,
their freedom made them happy;
and Christmas was a big surprise,
no turkey meat for Pappy.

Now celebrating with some pork,
the festive meal is keen;
as pigs can't fly, can hardly walk,
the knife is sharp and mean.

The squealing pigs will get revenge,
and find the turkey's nest!
injustice they will soon avenge,
as turkey meat's the best.

Turkish Delights

Floral allurement
leak perfumed peony scents—
pink Turkish delights

Peonies are one of the oldest known cultivated blooms tended by humans for at least 4,000 years for their medicinal purposes, wonderful aromas and pleasing appearance. A great number of them grow naturally in Turkey in the Caucasus mountains.

Under the Church Bells

And the sound of the chorus song haunts,
as the Church filled with history taunts;
and the primeval bells sounding loud—
tend to banish a troubled black cloud.

Still my ancestors speak from the grave,
in the books that I've read of the brave;
though the town concentrates on the past—
and the future's not promised to last.

As the cycle of life never ends,
and new people will try to set trends;
we will always forget those now dead—
as the new-borns have taken our bed.

So I bury my head in the sand,
and hope to belong to the land
when I'm slowed down by ageing old bones,
then I'll die in my pretty fine robes.

Ungratefulness

The bitter sharp enduring pain, ungratefulness exudes,
the dulling ache, another's wrath, and someone is abused;
unrecognising one's own flaws, as justice often fails,
and in its path are dead desires, as ego tips the scales.

Some never learn to gift a smile or offer helping hands,
and so bereft are those around with scuppered happy plans;
the sabotage is evident in spiteful cunning deeds
that cage a lion in its den so that it never feeds.

The rage of others shocks the one who never took the time
to see their own behaviour steal another's striving climb;
the lessons learned when we are young that sharing is a gift,
this means we have to understand that others will be miffed.

The bitter sharp enduring pain, ungratefulness extends,
relieve the ache, another's pain, on gratitude depends;
in recognising one's own flaws, lets justice shine within,
we give your thanks to those who want to let the fun begin.

Unseated by Treachery

Discredited by those who had the power to disgrace,
the mob had no integrity, they want to win the race;
so lies and rumour stirred a war of thoughtless tribal trouble,
and soon enough the chaos burst another's perfect bubble.

And no one could believe that such a deed could do much harm,
but jealousy and prejudice can be disguised as charm;
the aftermath of bullying can leave a trail of sorrow
defeating with an air of mournful grief to kill tomorrow.

But rising like a phoenix from the rubble of despair,
can thwart the mob who started up this torrid, sad affair;
experience is keen, as we must learn to quell the wave,
forget the pain of jealousy and rise above the grave.

For those who wish to take away our shine, do not deserve
to keep our company, or gain the right to be observed;
and pity is the only word that truly can describe,
a person who with treachery will take a dirty bribe.

Venice

A chart is painted from the start,
on every corner Venice scores;
you feel the heart within the town—
it's beat performs in perfect art.

A gown of riches draped around
in subtle swirls of coloured homes;
inside a crown of jewelled scenes,
designer stones renowned.

It seems this place is in my dreams,
I know it does exist, it's real—
fine precious themes of golden thread,
and you will feel its sunny beams.

(A Cryptic Labyrinth)

Vote with Care

Double trouble in the rubble,
arguments in parliaments;
aftermath can be a struggle,
sorting out the documents.

Stirring pots to start the plotting,
lies, deceit, essential heat;
fires are lit, there is no stopping,
cauldrons boil, the meat is sweet.

Heads will roll, the one controlling—
points the gun and we will run;
voting means there's no consoling
once in office, life's undone!

Please beware when you're declaring,
choose a guy or gal who'll try;
not a wuss who isn't daring,
half asleep— about to die.

(A Hectic Heptad)

Vultures

The Vultures pick the bones of those
who leave their wealth behind;
the thieving relatives who chose
to pilfer all they find.

The scavengers will ruthlessly
put jewels in their pocket;
hide and steal so shamelessly
take precious rings and locket.

Until the bone is dry and clean
and flavourlessly cold;
in heartless acts they're very mean
and keen to sell their gold.

The memories are left to die
a lifetime buried deep
there is no tear or saddened cry,
or loving word to keep.

The vultures have no conscience here
they think they have a right;
and so their job is very clear
not one of them contrite.

Walking the Dog

Man's best friend, we're always tending,
to their care, we must prepare;
in return their loyal friending—
bonds us so that we can share.

Dogs are pets that need protecting,
caring cheer they want to hear;
we just love that interjecting
jumping, running, it is clear . . .

shadows on the wall becoming
memories are remedies;
bonding as we keep on running,
life is full of melodies.

(A Hectic Heptad)

Walking the Mile

Encouraging are words I tell myself
to not be fazed by trouble when it comes;
be strong and steadfast, take care of my health,
and not be fooled by those who beat their drums.

Rely upon my faith, and on my wisdom,
remembering that tomorrow brings the light,
and sometimes one can't argue with the system,
to navigate the rules, stand-up and fight.

But then I tell myself to rest a while,
to take it easy, early to my bed--
the road is long and when I walk the mile,
it's good to have a clear, determined head.

Be in control, and carefully decide,
pragmatic too, reality can chide.

(A Sonnet)

Walking Warriors

The soldiers were starving and on their last legs
and turned into vagrants, for hunger still begs;
they walked until many had died on the way,
and hoped that tomorrow was brighter and gay.

The war could be over, they did not have news,
remaining still captive and some without shoes,
survival was paramount, living was key,
and thoughts of a time when they shared cups of tea.

When dropping like flies, they were shot in the head,
as life was so easily held by a thread,
and nothing would stop them from singing a song,
to lift up their spirits they all went along.

And when relief came, they would hear a kind voice
selections of food with a wonderful choice.
The troops were soon met with an allied brigade
American troops had arrived to invade.

At last they were saved, as the Germans retreated
a moment in time that would not be repeated,
the war was now over and they all went home,
and hardships of wartime would never be known.

We all Make Mistakes

As nobody is perfect, then I can accept my fate,
when making errors daily, then I will not get irate.
So many overlook a date, or word misspelt in print,
and once mistakes are on the wall, we have to take the hit.

And every now and then we spot a blunder or a fault,
and eager eagle eyes will zoom and give us all a jolt!
And there it is the one thing I've been searching for all day
a flaw that I can shout about, an oversight to slay.

And even fresh new eyes can miss an error on the page,
embarrassing to see a printed slip-up on the stage;
at least it was detected soon before the public saw
the poster with an error in the date we can't ignore.

Weather Wishes

Blue,
the sky will come to mind for me--
a tranquil sea reflects the tint,
a hue that brings a guarantee
that cloud will take a subtle hint . . . .

and let the azure filter down,
to take away my sulky frown.

(A Peppered Pickle)

Wedding Day In Venice

Excitement fills the atmosphere,
in Venice love can dance—
her gown of chiffon floating free
with passion and romance.

A picture perfect bridal scene
on gondolas they ride;
the buildings here fit for a Queen,
creative art applied.

Surrounded by Venetian colour
Every where's in vogue
in Italy the days of summer
flush with precious gold.

As wedding bells ring out aloud,
and celebrate today;
inside the chapel where they vowed,
'til death they'll always stay.

Welcoming Solitude

The intermittent silent mood
began to speak of solitude;
a state I knew would soon unfold
prepared was I for something cold.
I never felt afraid of it,
I knew that you could not commit
and knowing this would change tomorrow
I refused to feel such sorrow.

As solitude has been a friend
and I prefer it in the end--
the peace without a single sound
begins to soothe and be profound . . .
as silence has a pleasant ring,
I feel a tranquil soothing spring;
a touching slowing of real time
where I can write a happy rhyme.

Whaling

For whale oil they set sail— harpooning monsters out at sea,
to fill their barrels, courage reigned, the battle set them free—
the power of these blowing mammals, fought like ocean dogs,
and blood was spilt by man at sea just like the pigs and hogs.
The meat was sold, the oil was cold, and trading was their game,
as whaling was a crying shame, when victory is claimed.

Then came the day the ship far out had spotted something white,
the Offshore grounds, a big great white had splashed his tail in flight,
among the fields of flukes he swam as free as any bird,
to tackle something quite this big— ambitions were absurd.
But man would not be beaten by a fish of any size—
their only thought was capturing the biggest fishing prize.

They set the sails and headed out to where they saw the beast—
and harnessing a catch like this would haul a major feast;
the alabaster demon was one hundred feet in length—
a sight they would remember, as this whale was Heaven sent;
each man was armed with spears and ropes, to bring the Devil home—
the skirmish sloshed and tossed the sea, creating frothing foam.

The tiny boat was soon upturned, the men swam for their lives,
a gaping jaw had opened wide, and swallowed them inside;
the vengeful whale surrounded all the men aboard the ship—
he swam beneath the hull and then the bow began to tip,
the vessel was soon on its side and men were floating near,
a feast was made of all of them, their knuckles white with fear.

What's Good for the Goose

You might think that you are the boss,
but listen here to me;
as just because you where brown socks,
there is no guarantee.

And we demand respect, d'you hear?
as we will have our say;
no need to shed an anxious tear,
as we can run away.

Us girls, we are a fine brigade,
and we can be hostile;
so if you want your supper made,
then give us all a smile!

What Happened to Silence

The underlying hum of man,
creating noisy chaos;
the thumping, jumping all began,
with motors to annoy us.

Mechanical, electrical,
machines we build with pride;
the white noise, a direct result—
there is nowhere to hide.

And in the peaceful countryside
a tractor ploughs the field,
and drowns the sound of birds that tried
to sing, as engines squealed.

No matter where you live on earth,
you'll hear a noisy pound,
a screaming motor giving birth
with sound that's always loud.

What's up with Tup?

She stood on the corner and lit up a ciggy—
the chill in the air never stopped business;
confident and assured she knew her trade,
punters were her bread and butter.

Cars pulled up and she leaned in—
negotiation was brief, money first
leather seats are always cold
and men in suits even colder.

The exchange was as swift as blue chip stock
the price always varied depending on the mood,
today was a good day
and the deed slipped up and down like a silk stocking,
another satisfied customer paid he tab.

This good looking girl was no fool—
she knew men's needs and fulfilled them,
toffs in swanky cars were all the same to her,
they paid and she stayed.

Back home she counted the takings
and banked the cash— just another day at the office.

Who Knows?

Who knows what haunts a complex mind;
or makes us kind or hateful?
And can a face be undermined
by character, unfaithful.

We breathe and live in fam'ly tribes,
we're moulded by our scenes.
What does it take change our vibes,
to turn our faith to schemes?

Can wisdom bring about some peace
for those who suffer strife?
Some never feel that light release,
enjoy fulfilling life.

Who knows what haunts a complex mind
or touches hearts within;
and honesty escapes the blind
who dwell on pain and sin.

Wing Walking

A crazy hobby taking to the skies on wings of planes,
the terror of the flight can bring some fear within those veins;
forever pushing boundaries, where skies no longer limit,
these brave, courageous people seem to squander every minute.

The danger in this practice as there is no guarantee
survival on the edge of pilot's skill to some degree;
and crashing down to earth, the rider will be so exposed
to injuries and death if this ride dived upon its nose.

We challenge death and look into the face of fearful horror,
to ride outside the plane up in the air without a cover!
Is this the madness of those men who dice with life and win?
Or is this just another silly game played on a whim.

I know for certain I refuse to ride with devils high,
as life is much too precious just to lose it in the sky!
But watching men and women strap themselves to wings on planes,
reminds me that the human race will never be in chains.

Witches Brewing

A witch can smell out children when they're hiding under beds,
they like to fly with bats and tease those spiders in their webs.
They stir a brew of mischief in a cauldron filled with trouble—
their long and pointed finger nails will often burst your bubble.

The magic can be dark and cats observe a spell that's spun
and even snakes and lizards never have the chance to run.
A silhouette is seen at night, against the brightest moon—
a figure in a pointed hat is riding on a broom.

When witches get together, they have power in their hands
and whosoever enters their domain— are slaughtered lambs;
beware the coven will devour your spirit and your soul—
you may think you are strong, but you will lose your self-control.

A spell will put you in a trance and stir up petulance,
cantankerous are witches, and they can be perilous;
October means it's Halloween, have fun, and make the switch,
and scare the neighbours late at night by dressing as a witch.

Witches Gossip

The whispers in the back room,
where the rumours fly like bats—
the vampires of the night are where
the cliques wear tall black hats;
those witches on their broomsticks
stir the cauldron in their coven,
and spread a tale about the one
to victimise and govern.

They vow to stay together and
will save their accolades—
for those who sign in blood must then,
be faithful to crusades;
as loyalty's a must if you're
to rise above the crowd,
Machiavelli rules and
licking boots is what they've vowed.

The brew is stirred as anger's served
along with spite and snot,
the bitches will intend to stain
your soul with every plot;
and once the spell is cast, there is
no changing what they think,
as rumour is believed, and they
will cause a mighty stink!

This tight knit group of witches
conjure hell upon the night,
they fly up to the sky and target
those who will not fight;
by poking them with wicked words,
they never learn to write,
relying on their evil deeds,
pretend to be polite.

But we know who you are my dears,
the covenant of witches
who stick together in a brood
and cook up in their kitchens;
no matter what you say or do,
you have no clout in here,
so keep your Godless, rotten thoughts,
we know you're insincere.

Wolfio + Deerilet

The cunning wolf just loved to dance,
his heart was lost in sweet romance;
he clean forgot that he was feared,
by farmers, he was not revered.

He fell in love with Doe the deer
she fluttered lashes at him clear;
instead of hunting as he should
his heart was lost inside the wood.

At night they met and kissed 'till dawn,
he loved his gentle lady fawn;
she felt protected by the wolf,
the two would marry if they could.

But as with Shakespeare's Juliet
the two should not have really met;
this match would end in bitter tears
as wolves and deer encouraged sneers.

They made a pact to wed that night,
the moon was full and shining bright;
but when the farmer saw the wolf
he shot him dead, and understood . . .

he was a threat to all he had
and now the deer was very sad.
She cried as she was all alone
and met a pack of wolves at home.

Both wolf and deer no longer kiss,
and there would be no wedded bliss;
like Romeo and Juliet
their love was filled with much regret.

Word Play

As tongue and lips in harmony can speak a word or two,
and choosing is the privilege we own;
as wisely we select to make them dance in poems true,
and every time we write, we pick a bone.

Communication habits have a tendency to note
a ritual of common words in use;
extending our vocabulary into words that quote
a different approach that may seduce.

So twist the tongue, contort the lips, produce a unique write,
and tantalise with colourful new words;
to ruffle senses, tickle minds and give us all a fright!
As risky words will bring you good returns.

Worry Worms

Will worry ever leave our mind at rest,
as we prioritise— to fight the fire;
so many obstacles, we can protest,
anxiety will not let us retire.

There's always trouble churning inside you—
relaxing is the privilege of babes;
accepting change is something that we do,
more difficult it is with mounting age.

Remember every path we take is worn—
as others have been there, and know our pain;
decisions made may leave us weak and torn,
but rainbows colour skies behind the rain.

Imagine life without a future plight—
how boring life would be without a fight.

(A Sonnet)

Writers Tempt with Silent Words

Portrayed in art upon the page without a word we speak,
in images presented in a colourful critique—
a story of emotion, in a garden full of trees,
a winsome breeze, a sky of blue, a terrible disease . . .

we only need a thought, a sense of smell, a sight or sound,
and with the constant flow of ink, our words can be profound.
Poetic or in prose, we spread a whisper that is read—
reflect the past, predict a future time or place instead.

We have a world of seas and lands, we have no limits here—
just choose a subject, use your heart and let there be a cheer;
we take a new perspective on an old and tired scene—
and paint a picture with our words to tempt, we are so keen.

We bring new life to ancient words that have been used before,
when long ago they told a tale of love and grief and war;
and still today our words work hard to bring a tear to eyes,
in books and magazines our stories summon weepy cries.

And once the page is stained with thoughts that twirl inside our head
alive and kicking is our tale of torture and of dread;
we bring the truth and fantasy to entertain the crowd,
and every word read silently is singing out aloud.

Year of the Rabbit

The rabbit symbolises luck as plucky he can be,
his calm and peaceful character and curiosity—
means he avoids a fight and specialises in good taste
and never lets a lettuce leaf in gardens go to waste.

He's merciful and quiet and he never makes a fuss,
and beauty is skin deep, as he will never swear or cuss;
he symbolises mercy, with a graceful elegance,
the rabbit shines this year, with his artistic relevance.

In the Chinese culture, the rabbit is known to be the luckiest out of all the twelve animals. It symbolises mercy, elegance, and beauty. People who are born in the year of the rabbit are calm and peaceful. They avoid fighting and arguing at all times, they are artistic and have good taste in life.

You've Joined the Teen Club

Today you have become a teen,
you've joined the stylish women's team;
this means that you have earned a place,
inside the club we all embrace.

But there are rules you have to learn,
don't let this be a big concern,
and number one all ladies know,
do not be dull, but always glow.

To radiate the kind of heat
from smiles that never can be beat,
retain a certain charm inside—
and take your time when you decide.

Be firm with bullies full of sin,
they cheat, so never let them in;
be wise, don't ever tell a lie,
and always test before you buy.

And keep your Mum quite close at hand,
as she will always understand;
if someone breaks your precious heart
then listen to your Mum, she's smart.

Remember I am always here,
and if you need support my dear—
I'll come and show the way to stay
beside a sunbeam every day.

For Isabella on her 13th birthday.

The Author's Biography

Christine was born in Birmingham, in the United Kingdom, where she has spent most of her life. Her passion and love of poetry started at college when she was lucky enough to have her first poem published, 'The Beach", at the age of seventeen. Since then she has developed her talent for rhyming words, and many more poems have been published on Amazon, Forward Poetry, The United Press and Local Publications. Her poems have also won contests on Fanstory.com.

She is pleased to present "Poetic Reflections"

Other recent poetry books include:

Dickens' Characters in Rhyme	-	A fully illustrated colour Poetry book
Spirited Sonnets	-	A collection of 160 traditional Sonnets
Glimpsing Light in Poetry	-	500 Poems with b/w illustrations
300 Soulful Sonnets	-	A Shakespearean Sonnet Collection
101 Poetic Personalities from History		A full colour book of famous faces
A Plethora of Poignant Poetry	-	200 Poems with b/w illustrations
The Fascinating World of POETIC Bugs	-	100 Poems with full colour illustrations
The Poetic Philosophy of Life	-	130 Poems with b/w illustrations
POETIC Bird Watch	-	A full colour book of birds
POETIC Flowering Blossom	-	A full colour book of flowers
Nature's Poetic Chimes	-	A full colour nature book
The Awdl Sonnet	-	Dedicated to the Awdl Sonnet form
The Awdl Gynt	-	Poems dedicated to a welsh poetry form

All available on Amazon.com

She originally worked as an aerobics fitness instructor for local authority gyms around Birmingham, and also Aston University, before retiring.

The inspiration for this book comes from personal experiences of love and loss, emotions, reflections and challenges in daily life. The influence of nature on our world and environment is profound and our inner peace and calm is the result of good thoughts and a positive attitude. Admiration and appreciation for others, including wildlife, enhances one's feeling of well-being. The joys of life are free, if we just open our eyes to them. My muse is the pleasure of life itself, the power to survive is strong in all creatures on earth.

Welcome to: Poetic Reflections

Life is Short

The early evening shadows cast a spell upon the earth,
as skies are lit with fiery auburn just about to birth;
another day is done and memories are set in stone,
and in the park the silhouettes of widows walk alone.

The years have aged as time is unforgiving in its step,
the seasons came and went before the eye could intercept;
a running pace replaced the early youthful years of old,
and only left a trace of life that was once pure as gold.

The saddest truth is that our fleeting moments never last,
a second flashes by and then it rests inside the past;
we are on borrowed time as everyone returns to earth
as life is short and we begin to die from every birth.

Christine Burrows

MMXIV

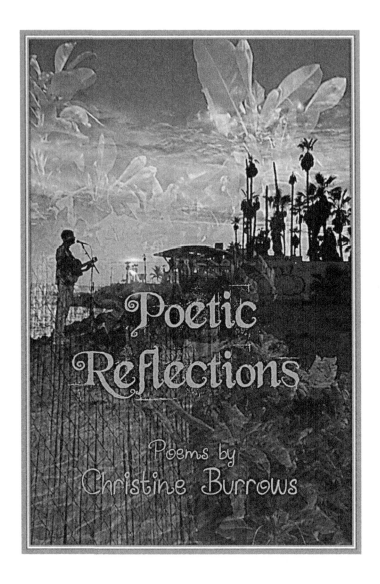

Poetic Reflections

Poems by
Christine Burrows

Printed in Great Britain
by Amazon